FACTORY-ORIGINAL
WARTIME JEEPS

FACTORY-ORIGINAL
WARTIME JEEPS

Originality guide to Willys MB and Ford GPW Jeeps

BY JAMES TAYLOR
PHOTOGRAPHY BY SIMON CLAY

Herridge & Sons

Published in 2020 by
Herridge & Sons Ltd
Lower Forda, Shebbear
Beaworthy, Devon EX21 5SY

Reprinted 2024

© Copyright James Taylor 2020

Design: Muse Fine Art & Design

All rights reserved. No part of this publication may be reproduced in any form or by any means without the prior written permission of the publisher and the copyright holder.

ISBN 978-1-906133-94-8
Printed in China

CONTENTS

INTRODUCTION 6

THE WARTIME JEEP 8

BODY & FITTINGS 22

LIGHTING & ELECTRICS 42

DASH & INTERIOR 50

ENGINE & TRANSMISSION 66

CHASSIS, SUSPENSION, WHEELS 80

ADDITIONS 92

APPENDIX A – BRITISH JEEPS 103

APPENDIX B – THE HOTCHKISS M201 108

INTRODUCTION

This book is intended to give Jeep enthusiasts and restorers an idea of what is "correct" for their vehicles, but it is important at the outset to recognise that only a tiny proportion of all preserved Jeeps are completely "correct". Most of those were discovered in as-supplied condition in shipping crates many years after the Second World War had ended, and had never been used.

In the field and in the motor pools, nobody cared whether the replacement part they were fitting was "correct" in terms of original factory specification. What mattered was that it would fit and would do the job – and that was precisely the point of the standardised specification that was drawn up for the Jeep. However much the design evolved over the four years it was in production, it had to be possible to use freshly delivered spares to revitalise an older model or to cannibalise a wrecked Jeep and use its parts for any number of others. As a result, most Jeeps probably ceased to be "correct" within a few weeks of entering active service.

All Jeep enthusiasts have to make a decision about what they want to achieve. Running and enjoying a generic Jeep with an amalgam of parts from different sources is quite enough for many people. Others focus on what is generally called a "motor pool" restoration, which aims to get the Jeep into a condition which it might have had while in service and after passing through the motor pool a few times to have damaged or worn parts replaced by whatever was available at the time. Only a few people aim for absolute factory authenticity, by which they mean that their vehicles have the exact specification with which they left the factory and before they entered the hurly-burly of service life. That is incredibly difficult to achieve, and it is also incredibly difficult to establish what that factory-fresh specification should be. Enthusiasts still argue happily (sometimes acrimoniously) over certain aspects of original specifications, 75 years after the last Jeep left the production lines.

Never let anybody tell you how your Jeep "should" be. Aiming for the impossible will take much of the fun out of Jeep ownership – and it is your Jeep, after all. The aim of this book is certainly not to tell you how your Jeep "should" be, but rather to give you an idea of how it probably was when new so that you can enjoy discovering the changes that have been made over its life and maybe get extra enjoyment from working out why those changes were made. Perhaps they were made in the field; perhaps they were made by somebody who wanted to use the vehicle as an everyday runabout after its war service was over; perhaps they were made by a previous owner who simply used whatever parts were readily available at the time.

Jeep research continues, and I have no doubt that it will do so for very many years yet. More information is coming to light all the time, and old theories are being replaced with new ones. The wartime Jeep remains an enduringly fascinating subject, and I hope that this book will help a few more people to understand why. It could not have been put together without the work already done by Jeep researchers and enthusiasts all around the world. I should single out particularly Lawrence Nabholtz's pioneering *The Military Jeep* (of which there have been both legal and illegal reprints) and John Farley's *The Standardised War-Time Jeep* (in its second, revised edition), and on the web it is always entertaining to follow new discoveries in the G503 Military Vehicle Message Forums at forums/g503.com. Many individuals have also provided additional information over the years which has found its way into this book, and I am grateful to all of them.

Special thanks go to photographer Simon Clay, who dug into his own collection of auction photographs and also chased around the country to photograph Jeeps owned by:

Henry Bennett	1942 Ford GPW
Paul Glennon	1945 Willys MB
Martin Graver	1942 Ford GPW
Ian Hollingsworth	1945 Ford GPW
Will Mann	1942 Willys MB
Bob Poplett	1944 Ford GPW
Richard Ravenscroft	1945 Ford GPW chassis
Keith Sherwood	1945 Ford GPW

Several photographs have also come from my own collection, including those of Mike Rivett's slat-grille Willys and Rodney Thompson's REME demonstration chassis.

James Taylor
Oxfordshire, June 2020

THE WARTIME JEEP

The increasing use of motor vehicles during WWI set the US military on a trajectory that eventually led to the vehicle known as a Jeep. As early as 1919, the US Quartermaster Corps recommended the acquisition of a new kind of military vehicle, "of light weight and compact size, with a low silhouette and high ground clearance, [which should also] possess the ability to carry weapons and men over all sorts of rough terrain."

No such vehicle yet existed, and without the imperative of a war none would be developed. But in 1935 the US Congress called for "remotorisation of the Army", recognising that it could not continue to rely on horse-drawn transport for ever and that its motley collection of motor vehicles left over from the First World War was hopelessly inadequate for any future conflict. Out of this grew a recognition that future military motor vehicles needed to be standardised, in order to improve spare parts logistics on the battlefield.

There had already been several trials with light motor vehicles that might be of use for liaison and reconnaissance duties, but none had been conclusive. Nevertheless, the US Infantry Board did take an interest in the British Army's use of the diminutive Austin 7 car as a reconnaissance vehicle. Though quite out of its depth in muddy terrain, the vehicle was light enough to be manhandled out of trouble in an emergency. It was also available in the USA, where it was manufactured under licence by a company called American Austin with headquarters in Butler, Pennsylvania. This company went bankrupt in 1938 and was re-organised as American Bantam, and that same year it provided three roadster models for military trials. The US Army declined to place an order for more, but maintained contact with American Bantam and discussed ideas for a new reconnaissance vehicle with them.

The next important decision was taken during 1939, when the US Army introduced a standardisation system for its general-purpose trucks that classified them by payload rating. The smallest size was a half-ton, but a year later the categories were revised and a new quarter-ton category was introduced while the half-ton category gave way to a ¾-ton class. The quarter-ton category would realistically be of minimal use as a load carrier, and was clearly intended to incorporate the light reconnaissance-type vehicle that the military did not yet have.

They soon would. War had broken out in Europe in autumn 1939 and, despite the traditionally insular stance of the USA and the reluctance of the American people to become embroiled in a foreign war, it was obvious to military commanders and clear-thinking politicians alike that the country would be dragged into the conflict before long. So it was that on 27 June 1940, the Ordnance Technical Committee of the US Quartermaster Corps (QMC) called for a new vehicle to fit that requirement for a quarter-ton model. It would have to have four-wheel drive to remain driveable in rough terrain, it would have to meet a stipulated weight limit, and it would have to satisfy certain other performance criteria.

It was all done in something of a rush. The Army had only been working seriously on its requirements for such a vehicle since the beginning of the month, and now it asked for proposals to be submitted by 22 July, giving interested parties less than a month to make up their minds. The request went out to no fewer than 135 companies across the USA.

The urgency was even more obvious in the follow-up request. Not only were interested parties asked to submit plans of their

The very first Bantam prototype, with designer Karl Probst standing at the back and, not surprisingly, looking a little weary.

proposals, but if they were really serious they also had to submit 70 finished prototypes for testing within 75 days after that, all produced at their own expense. The first prototype had to be submitted within 49 days, and the remainder within the 75-day time-frame. (Eight of those 70 prototypes had to have four-wheel steering to meet a US Cavalry requirement, which complicated the issue even further.)

Unsurprisingly, most of those invited to tender for the contract found this too difficult. In fact, only two companies even bothered to respond. These were American Bantam, and Willys-Overland of Toledo in Ohio. Like Bantam, Willys had been through a difficult period and had been through its own re-organisation in 1936. Perhaps both companies believed that a major US Army contract would be their road to a more secure future.

Nevertheless, the Bantam and Willys representatives who submitted their designs at the US Army's Camp Holabird test ground near Baltimore in July found that they were not alone. Crosley, another maker of small cars, and Ford had both sent representatives as observers, reasoning that they might stand a chance if the deadline had proved too tight for anyone else to come up with a design. Ford had probably had their corporate arm twisted by the QMC, who would have wanted to get access to the company's vast production capacity. Crosley, however, soon faded from the picture.

The Willys design was really little more than an outline

This was the Willys Quad. Just two were made to this specification.

This was the revised Bantam entry in its (limited) production guise as a BRC-40. This example saw service with the British 6th Armoured Division. (IWM photo)

FACTORY-ORIGINAL WARTIME JEEPS

The Willys MA that preceded the standardised MB had freestanding headlamps, a curved bonnet (hood) panel, and the Willys name prominently across its nose. This was a publicity shot of the time, showing the MA demonstrating its ability to climb and descend a flight of steps.

sketch, and the company wanted to extend the time allowed for building a first prototype. However, the Bantam proposal was well-executed and was complete. So even though Bantam's costs were higher than those proposed by Willys, the Quartermaster Corps favoured their proposal and asked them to go ahead and build the prototype batch of 70 vehicles. The first was delivered to Camp Holabird for testing on 23 September, just half an hour before the expiry of the deadline for its submission set by the Army.

This Bantam was to prove the basis for the eventual production Jeep, and it is a matter of record that it had been designed in two and a half days by a consulting engineer called Karl K Probst, whom Bantam had hired specifically for the job. It was based to a large extent on existing components, with a reinforced version of the same Bantam roadster chassis that had been submitted for military approval in 1938 and rejected. It had a bought-in Continental four-cylinder engine, and there were Spicer axles and transmission components. The doorless steel body tub was as basic as it could be, the front wings were little more than splash guards, and the weight was well above the limit set by the Quartermaster Corps because Probst had considered their demands unrealistic and had simply ignored them!

This first hand-built prototype proved capable of taking everything that the Army testers could throw at it. So impressed was the Quartermaster Corps that it placed an order for a further 1500 examples even before Bantam had completed the batch of 70 prototypes. These vehicles entered service – many with Allied forces as well as with the US Army – and were known as Bantam BRC-40s. Those initials stood for Bantam Reconnaissance Car, 40bhp (which was the output of the Continental engine).

However, the Quartermaster Corps had serious doubts about Bantam's ability to build the BRC-40 in the sort of volumes it had in mind. So Bantam stood by helplessly while the blueprints of its design – which under the terms of the contract had now become military property – were handed over to Willys and to Ford. Both of these companies now expressed an interest in building prototypes at their own expense, and by November 1940 examples of the Ford Pygmy and Willys Quad were on test at Camp Holabird alongside the Bantams. Their basic design borrowed heavily from Bantam's pioneering work, but each incorporated a number of changes and individual features.

In particular, each vehicle had its own maker's engine. The Ford Pygmy had a modified tractor engine, which was the only four-cylinder type the company then had in production, and it also had an elderly transmission that had originated with the Model A cars. The Willys Quad, however, had the latest version of its maker's Go-Devil side-valve four-cylinder engine that had been in production since 1926 and had most recently been updated by Chief Engineer Barney Roos for the Whippet saloon in 1938. With 63bhp, it offered much more power than either the Ford engine or the Continental type used in the Bantam, and it also came with a long pedigree of reliable service.

Like Bantam, both Ford and Willys were given contracts for 1500 vehicles. Ford came back with a modified vehicle that it called the GP (General Purpose), which was not helped by having the same old tractor engine and antiquated transmission. Despite the excellence of its engine, the Willys Quad was well over the weight limit specified by the Quartermaster Corps, and so Willys were instructed to cut its weight down dramatically

> **THE JEEP MA**
> The Willys model MA followed on from the original Quad prototypes and earned a contract for 1500 examples from the US Army. Exact figures are disputed, but many experts accept that a total of 1555 examples were built between June and September 1941, before Willys production changed over to the standardised MB. These MA Jeeps carried serial numbers between 78401 and 79907.
>
> Fewer than 30 of these early iterations of the wartime Jeep are now believed to survive world-wide.

THE WARTIME JEEP

The first version of the Willys MB was the slat-grille, so called because of the fabricated grille seen on this well-worn but much loved example. Like all Jeeps, it just keeps on going, nearly 80 years after it was made.

for their 1500 "production" vehicles. They did so – and the result was the Willys MA, which was actually considerably different from the Quad prototypes originally submitted for testing.

By this stage in the proceedings, the QMC's preference was already clear, and when the final tests were run between a Willys MA, a Ford GP and a Bantam BRC-40, no-one was very surprised to see the Willys come out as a clear winner. Bantam had to be content with second place, and Ford came a poor third. So on 23 July 1941 – a year and a day after the original deadline for expressions of interest in the quarter-ton contract – Willys was awarded a contract to build 16,000 further revised models, which quite logically became known as the MB type.

That was not quite that, however. The QMC still had concerns about production capacity, which may have been greater at Willys than at Bantam but was still nowhere near big enough for the huge quantities of vehicles that the US Army was likely to need. So further orders were placed for the intermediate designs in order to make a start on providing US Army units with the new quarter-ton model. Willys appears

A good, honest and enjoyable Jeep. Basically a 1942 model, Henry Bennet's GPW has been restored to look the part rather than to factory-fresh condition. The hood number is that of an aircraft that was shot down over the owner's house in wartime Suffolk, and the markings are those of the 448th Bomb Group that was based in Britain.

to have built a few more of its MA; Bantam was given a supplementary order for another 2674 BRC-40 models, this time to an improved MkII design, but subsequently bowed out of the programme. Ford built around another 2000 of its GP models before swallowing its corporate pride and agreeing to build the Willys MB under licence in its own factories. So it was that on 10 November 1941, the company was awarded an initial contract for a further 15,000 of what it called the Ford GPW. Those letters stood for General Purpose – Willys.

The new vehicle needed a better name. It must have been obvious that the average US GI was never going to distinguish between Willys MB and Ford GPW – or care that the vehicle was dual-sourced, for that matter. Various options were tried and failed to catch on, but the name that did emerge was probably coined somewhere within the US Army. That name was Jeep. Was it a contraction of the letters GP for General Purpose? Was it a fashionable description of the time for

something otherwise nameless? Nobody knows for certain, but it was a name that rapidly gained currency. It was certainly in use by February 1941, when it appeared in an article published in the *Washington Daily News* that was widely syndicated elsewhere.

The Jeep that went into full volume production was really an amalgam of Bantam, Willys and Ford ideas. In broad terms, its basic design was by Bantam and its engine was by Willys. Yet it also had details that had originated with Ford. Most notable among these was the flat bonnet, which was altogether much more practical as a mobile table than the rounded design on the Willys MA. Most importantly, the production models were thoroughly standardised: Willys parts would fit Ford-built Jeeps and vice versa.

None of that prevented the two companies making their own improvements to the design as they went along, always ensuring that they met the military requirement for complete interchangeability. Willys, as the smaller company, bought many parts in from outside suppliers and tended not to ask for specification changes because these cost money. Ford, on the other hand, was able to make far more of the Jeep's components in-house, and over the years would make a number of minor changes that simplified production or reduced costs. Perhaps not wishing to come off second best, Ford stamped its company logo (a stylised, script "F") into almost every component that it made, and into some that it bought in as well. Even nuts and bolts were Ford-branded, and it would not have upset Ford to discover that some of them ended up on Willys Jeeps as motor pools maintained and rebuilt Jeeps with whatever came to hand.

Most of this book is devoted to the differences of detail that occurred on production over the years, but it is possible to pick out a few key points in order to understand the broader picture. Willys, of course, had a head start over Ford because they started production in October 1941 and had already built well over 8000 MB Jeeps by the time Ford production began in January 1942. In that time, there had already been one very obvious change to the specification, when the windscreen frame had changed in December 1941 from the type used on the MA (with a shallow panel below the glass) to the standardised type (with a much deeper panel).

Although a standardised specification existed by the end of 1941, it continued to evolve in the first six or seven months of 1942 in the light of changing needs and new ideas. So although Willys entered 1942 building "slat-grille" models, with a radiator grille made from several slats welded together that was ultimately derived from the Bantam design, Ford redesigned this from the start to a simple pressed panel. It was an idea typical of Ford production engineering, and such a sensible one that Willys adopted it from March 1942.

All Ford GPWs were also built with a lidded glove-box in the dash, giving the Jeep's users somewhere to stow small items of equipment (although the US Army of course had its own ideas about what should be stowed there). Willys adopted this on production in February 1942. That month, both manufacturers changed from the original solid-disc wheels to split-rim "combat" wheels, which simplified tyre changing in the field.

From the beginning of MB production, Willys had stamped their brand name in large letters into the rear panel of the Jeeps they built. Not to be outdone, Ford stamped theirs in a similar position from the start of GPW production. However, the US Quartermaster Corps decided to ban the practice, which they saw as not conducive to the purpose of the Jeep, and insisted that these blatant brand advertisements were discontinued. So from approximately July 1942, both Willys and Ford introduced plain tail panels, and the early bodies have since become known as "script" types.

Summer 1942 brought some further changes, and one of the more obvious was the standardisation of a blackout driving light on the left-hand front wing (fender). It arrived during July on Willys models and during August on Fords. But the major change in this period was all but invisible, and it involved minimising the amount of rubber used in the Jeep. The Japanese invasion of the Far East early in 1942 had led to a rubber shortage in the USA, and inevitably there had to be cutbacks. Multiple minor items that had earlier been made of rubber were replaced by items made of materials such as felt, or were simply left off altogether. Over the autumn of that year, the rubber seals around the tail light units disappeared, for example; the steering-wheel was redesigned with metal spokes and a different compound for its moulded rim; and the seats lost their rubber cushions in favour of felt over steel springs.

The adjustments to the standard specification continued in August 1942 when a jerrycan bracket was added to the tail panel, enabling Jeeps to carry just over 5 US gallons of extra fuel, which was good for 80 miles or more on tarmac roads. (The jerrycan was actually copied from a German design that held 20 litres, and its name reflects its origin: "Jerry" was Second World War slang for German.)

By this stage, the standardised Jeep was very much fit for purpose, but modifications continued as more and more uses were developed. So from March 1943, the focus was on modifications that would enable more Jeeps to be used as radio communications vehicles. Rather than develop two types of Jeep, the solution was to fit all production models with a basic level of essential equipment and allow units in the field to install the radio sets if they needed them. As a result, a radio junction box became standard, and over the next few months there were progressive improvements to the suppression arrangements.

The bonnet numbers give away that this impressive picture of Jeeps awaiting delivery shows Willys models that were built in July 1942.

FACTORY-ORIGINAL WARTIME JEEPS

Displaying several additions to the original specification, this 1942 Ford has a pedestal mount and rifle rack within the body, a surge tank at the front and decontaminator on the wing, and is towing a quarter-ton trailer typical of those used behind Jeeps during the conflict.

The no-frills interior of the standardised Jeep is clear in this picture of a 1942 GPW. Martin Graver has restored this one twice over a period of 40 years, and it now features a PTO-driven 12-volt generator between the front seats, among other interesting additions.

THE WARTIME JEEP

Jeeps were expected to carry anything and everything, and they still do. This one displays a radio antenna mount, a radio, a hand winch, and a canvas cover for field eating utensils – among other things.

There were various attempts to produce sidescreens that would weatherproof the Jeep, some of them improvised in the field. This Willys MB was built in June 1942, although the sidescreens may be much later.

FACTORY-ORIGINAL WARTIME JEEPS

Bob Poplett's 1944 GPW has been restored with the markings of the RAF. The canvas top always looked handsome when erect, although it was a deliberately simple and functional design.

A rear view of the same vehicle: the Jeep was never styled in the accepted sense, but it just looked right from the start.

Further changes were made during 1943. The crude manually-operated windscreen wipers were changed in August to a tandem system, which at least allowed the front-seat passenger to operate the wipers while the driver focussed more fully on driving. A month later, a rifle holder became standard, keeping a weapon within easy reach of the Jeep's occupants and formalising a common field modification. The biggest change, however, resulted from a major re-organisation of production arrangements. Ford stopped making Jeep bodies at their Lincoln plant in October 1943, in order to devote the space to other war matériel, and began instead to use Willys-pattern bodies supplied by the American Central Manufacturing Company. Despite the high degree of standardisation that had been achieved, this led to a problem: Ford ancillaries sometimes did not fit the Willys bodies. As a result, the bodies were redesigned as a "composite" type (often known as a Type 2 body), with elements of the Ford and Willys types, and both manufacturers used these on production from January 1944.

There were just two more major changes before production

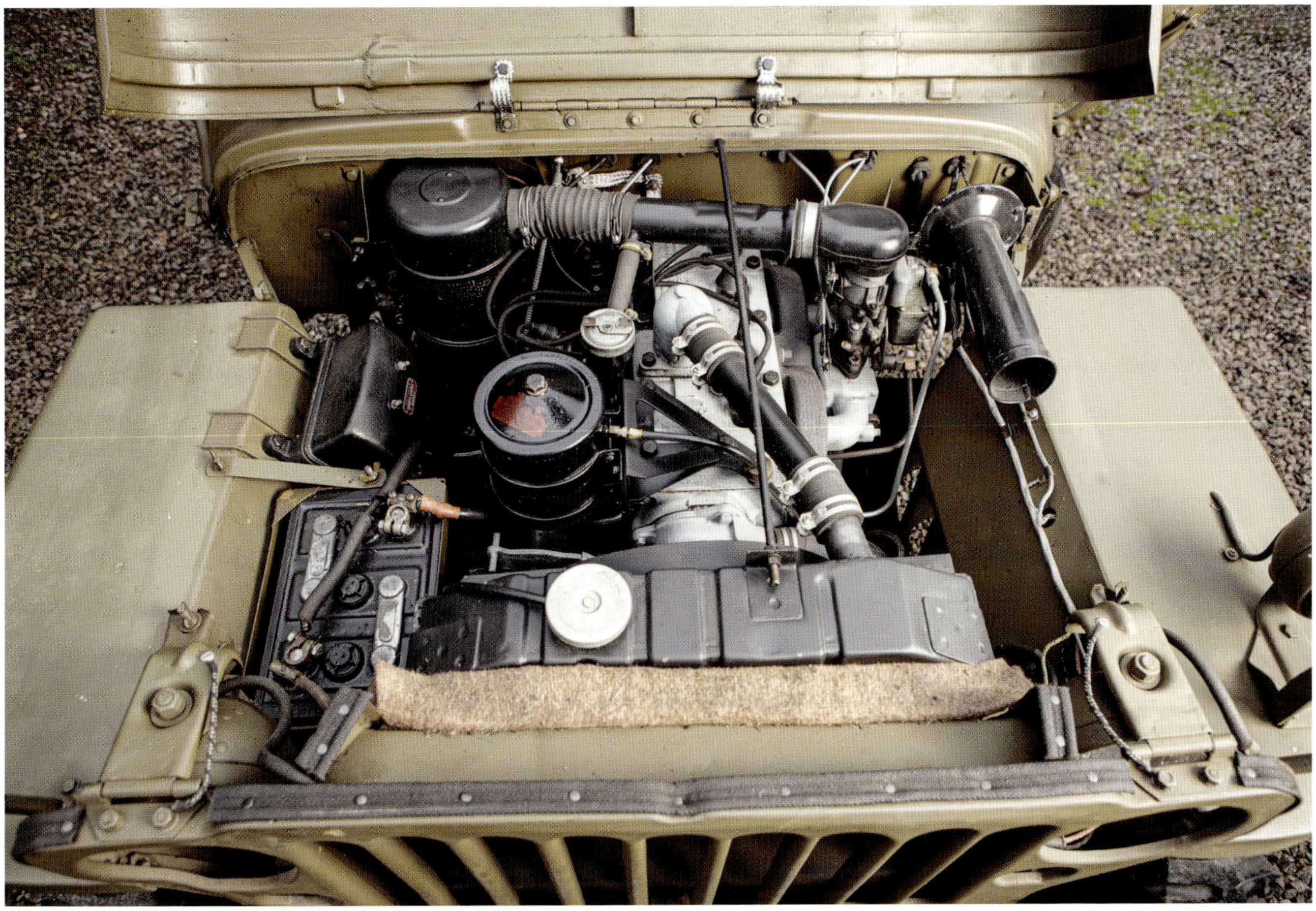

THE WARTIME JEEP

This late Ford engine bay has been kept as close as possible to factory specification. Note the extra earth braiding associated with late models.

Pretty much as supplied by the factory, this 1945 Jeep shows the sheer simplicity of the fittings, instruments and controls, as well as the hand-operated wipers used until very late in production.

Markings were mostly stencilled, like these on a 1945 Jeep. Earlier factory-applied markings were blue rather than white.

stopped in 1945. The first of these was confined to Willys models, and was a change from an internal expanding parking brake to an external contracting type. Ford continued production with

THE FORD GPA

The idea for an amphibious quarter-ton vehicle followed not long after the Jeep had been commissioned for production. It came from the US Motor Transport Board, was overseen by the National Defence Research Committee, and called for a "QMC-4 1/4 Ton Truck Light Amphibian". The vehicle was intended for such tasks as reconnaissance in advance of river crossings and some types of amphibious landing assaults.

Yacht specialists Sparkman & Stephens of Newport, Rhode Island, were given the job of designing a hull for the vehicle, along the lines of the one they had already drawn up for the much larger (and better known) DUKW. Two companies put forward manufacturing proposals. One was military vehicle manufacturer Marmon-Herrington, who planned a welded monocoque structure, and the other was Ford, whose design used a conventional chassis and an internal frame to which the outer hull cladding would be attached. The Ford proposal not only used as many elements as possible of the standardised GPW but was also around 400 lb lighter than the Marmon-Herrington.

Unsurprisingly, the Ford proposal was rewarded with the contract. The amphibious Jeep was given the designation GPA (General Purpose, Amphibian) and the first production-pattern vehicles began trials in February 1942, just as Ford were getting production of the GPW under way. There was considerable enthusiasm from US Army Generals for this new development, and this may explain why trials were not as thorough as they might have been. By April, Ford had received an order for the first 5000 examples of what would later be nicknamed the Seep (Seaborne Jeep).

The reality was that the GPA did not live up to expectations. With a weight of 3500 lb, it had become much heavier than the 2600 lb called for in the original design brief. This weight gave the GPA a very low freeboard in the water, with the results that its cargo-carrying ability was limited and that it could not cope with even small waves. GIs found it heavy and unwieldy, and the vehicle's specialist and therefore rather limited use offered very little opportunity for field experience to be fed back to the manufacturers to help improve the design. It required more maintenance than was ideal, and it was not until November 1942 that the first modifications were made to improve it.

They were not enough. Production was brought to an end in March 1943 after just 12,778 had been built. Although GPAs were used in the Sicily landings of September 1943, the majority of those built were sent to Russia under Lend-Lease arrangements. A total of 383 were also supplied to the British armed forces.

The GPA had a slightly longer wheelbase than a standard Jeep, with a dimension of 84 inches. It was powered by a standard Jeep engine and, as on the DUKW, the transmission's power take-off was used to power a screw-type propellor that ran in a tunnel faired into the underside of the rear body. There was also a rudder for directional control in the water.

The Ford GPA amphibian was closely related to the Jeep but was nowhere near as successful.

Ford's huge production resources were seen as essential, and the company was persuaded to build the Willys design under licence.

the earlier type until the end. Then from approximately May 1945, vacuum-operated windscreen wipers became standard on both Willys and Ford models.

Ford assembly of Jeeps ended during July 1945, and Willys assembly ended during September. Production of a peacetime model, the CJ-2A, had already started on the Willys lines in June, but Ford would have no more to do with the Jeep.

Willys had built a total of 359,489 MB Jeeps at their Toledo factory. Ford, starting production at the beginning of 1942, built 277,896 GPWs in six factories across the USA, using a seventh factory for body production up to October 1943. In addition, Willys had built 1555 of the early model MA and Ford had built 12,778 amphibious GPA variants of the GPW (see sidebar). By the end of the Second World War, the US Army calculated that it had 10 years' supply of new and unissued Jeeps stockpiled all over the country.

The Ford body plant was in Lincoln, Nebraska. The six assembly plants were at Chester in Pennsylvania, Dallas in Texas, Dearborn (River Rouge) in Michigan, Edgewater in New Jersey (which came on-stream in January 1943), Louisville in Kentucky, and Richmond in California. Although there was formidable standardisation throughout, the different Ford plants sometimes introduced new features at different times to one another, with the result that it is rarely possible to establish exact specification change points for Ford-built Jeeps. As all the Willys Jeeps were built at the same place, there is a much better understanding of production changeover points.

THE WARTIME JEEP

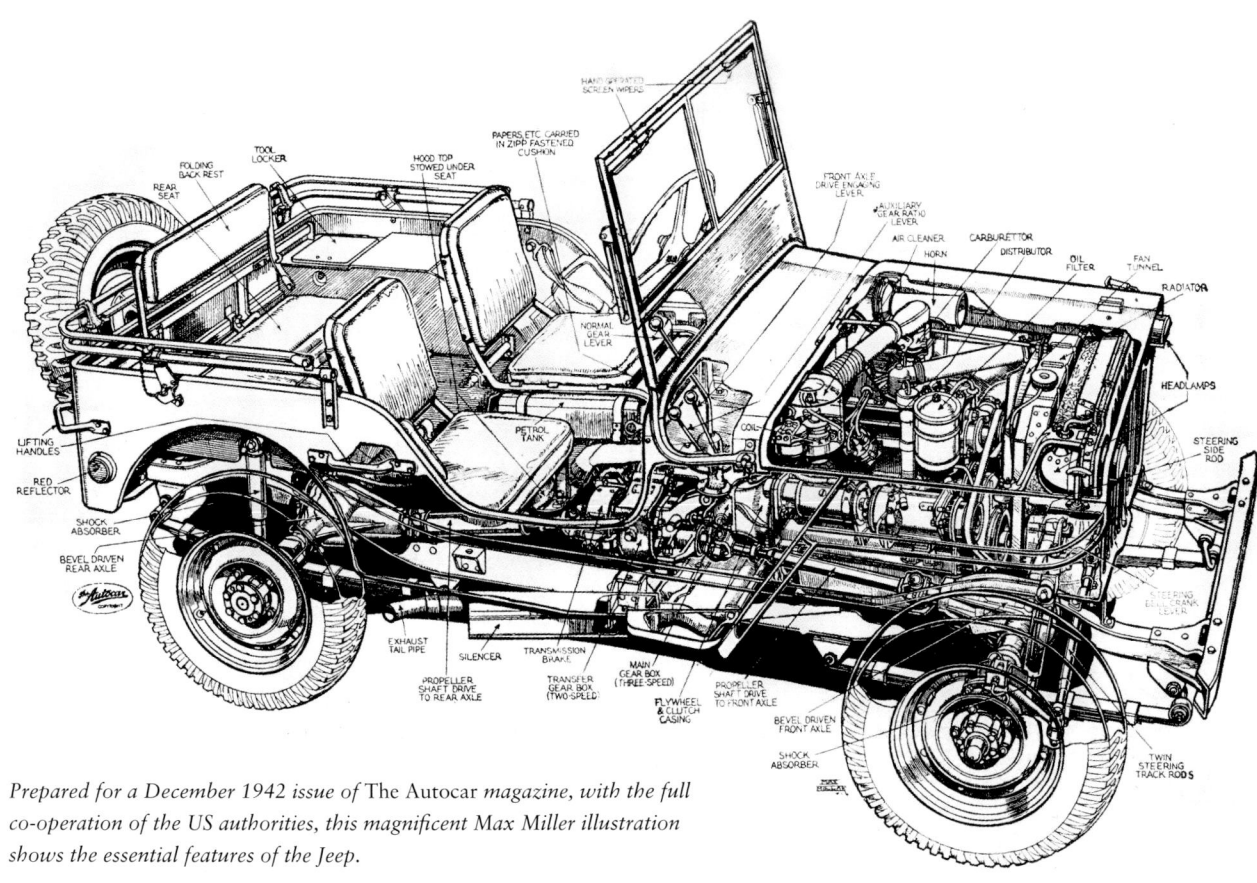

Prepared for a December 1942 issue of The Autocar *magazine, with the full co-operation of the US authorities, this magnificent Max Miller illustration shows the essential features of the Jeep.*

WILLYS MB AND FORD GPW – OUTLINE SPECIFICATIONS

Engine
Willys Go-Devil with cast-iron block and cylinder head
134.2 cu in with 3.125in bore and 4.375in stroke
(2199cc with 79.4mm bore and 111.1mm stroke)
L-head design with pushrod-operated valves and single chain-driven camshaft
Three-bearing crankshaft
Compression ratio 6.48:1
Carter 539 S single-barrel downdraught carburettor
60bhp at 3600rpm
105 lb ft at 2000rpm

Gearbox
Three-speed manual,
with synchromesh on second and third
Ratios 2.67:1, 1.56:1, 1.00:1, and 3.55:1 (reverse)

Axle ratio
4.88:1

Suspension
Front and rear suspension with semi-elliptic leaf springs and hydraulic shock absorbers

Steering
Cam and twin lever type with variable (12:1 to 14:1) ratio

Brakes
Drum brakes on all four wheels, with 9in diameter and hydraulic actuation; drum-type parking brake acting on rear transmission output shaft

Dimensions
Overall length: 122in/3350mm
Overall width: 62in/1600mm
Overall height: 69in/1750mm with canvas erected
Wheelbase: 80in/2030mm

Wheels and tyres
6.00 x 16in wheels with six-ply NDT tyres

Weights
Gross weight 3243 lb/1471kg (typical)
Payload 800 lb/363kg

Performance
Maximum speed 65mph
0-50mph 19 sec

FACTORY-ORIGINAL WARTIME JEEPS

Marked up with the M-prefix of a British Jeep, this 1942 model has seen multiple modifications over the years but again, looks the part and gives its owner a lot of enjoyment.

The foundation of every Jeep is this remarkably simple channel-section chassis. The one shown dates from 1945, but there were only detail changes over the years.

THE WARTIME JEEP

ALLIED JEEPS

Although the Jeep was initially designed for the US Army, many Jeeps were actually supplied to allied forces. The countries which received them were Britain, Canada, China, France and Russia. There is more about the Jeeps supplied to the British forces in Appendix A.

For shipment overseas (both to the Allies and to US forces), Jeeps were sometimes partially dismantled and put into wooden packing cases. There were many scams after the war, supposedly offering a military-surplus Jeep-in-a-crate at a bargain price, but in practice very few such finds were ever made. One Jeep that was supposedly found still in its crate in the early 1980s was a late 1943 Willys model with chassis number 280026. It was, of course, assembled into a running Jeep and then sold.

Jeeps were shipped in Single Unit Packs (SUPs) or less commonly in Twin Unit Packs (TUPs). Crating a Jeep was a costly and time-consuming process and of course the vehicle had to be re-assembled when it reached its destination. So Jeeps were only crated when absolutely necessary; for example, if their delivery involved a long sea voyage. In such cases, the crates allowed several to be stacked one above the other on deck while protecting them from the weather and salt water spray.

Every Jeep carried three data plates on the dashboard, and here they are on a late Ford GPW. Original plates are often missing or damaged; reproductions have been available for many years, although their quality has been variable!

Some enthusiasts enjoy collecting war surplus militaria to go with their Jeeps – and why not?

Typically, the tyred wheels would be removed from a fully-assembled Jeep and it would be placed in a wooden frame which formed the base of the crate. All the top hamper would be removed, along with the steering wheel, and this would be stowed in and around the Jeep's main body-chassis assembly. The wooden crate would then be built up around this.

BODY & FITTINGS

The Jeep body was always made as separate front and rear halves, which were then joined in the middle. The join, just below the "door" aperture on each side of the body, is readily visible. Bodies were mounted to chassis by means of rubber-bushed mountings, with some variation between early and late types.

The primary body manufacturer was American Central Manufacturing (ACM), who were based at Connersville in Indiana and had been known as Auburn Central Manufacturing when they fielded the initial request from Willys for Jeep bodies in volume. ACM became American Central Manufacturing in March 1942 and initially they built Jeep bodies only for Willys.

The first GPW Jeeps that Ford assembled actually had Willys-pattern bodies that were built by ACM. However, Ford did not take long to get its own Lincoln plant in Detroit ready to manufacture Jeep bodies, and from January 1942 Ford Jeeps began to come off the assembly lines with Ford-built bodies. Inevitably, there were minor differences from the bodies manufactured at ACM, mainly as a result of Ford's manufacturing practices. However, the two body types were very similar indeed, and there were no differences that would prevent components being interchanged in the field.

All this changed again towards the end of 1943. By that stage, Ford had become very heavily involved in producing war matériel, and a decision was taken to free up manufacturing resources by handing the whole body operation over to ACM. So Ford stopped building its own bodies in October 1943, and the Jeeps it built between then and January 1944 used standard Willys bodies, albeit with Ford bolt-on items.

However, it soon became clear that the standard Willys bodies were different enough from the Ford types to cause problems on the Ford production lines. So the solution was to design a composite body, consisting in broad terms of the rear of the Willys body and the front of the Ford type. To simplify manufacture, the redundant Ford presses were shipped to ACM, and all further wartime Jeeps had the same composite body, manufactured by ACM. This is often known as the Type 2 body; the earlier Willys bodies, in retrospect, became known as Type 1 bodies.

Note, though, that each manufacturer continued to add its own parts to these basic composite bodies, so that the completed bodies from Willys still differed from those completed by Ford. A typical difference was in the tool box lids, for which each maker had its own distinctive design.

Much more recently, the enthusiast market has been well served by reproduction body tubs from a number of aftermarket sources. It is only fair to say that some of these are of better quality than others.

BODY

The Jeep's body tub is made of low-carbon steel, in 16 gauge for the floorpan but in 18 gauge for all the superstructure. The join between front and rear sections is reinforced on the inside of the panels by a simple strengthening bracket on the earliest models. From February 1942 and MB 118600, that bracket was changed for a more substantial one that had a fish-tail shape.

The main differences between the early Willys bodies and the Ford ones are in the shape of the toeboard gussets, which are roughly triangular braces that run between the engine side of the bulkhead (firewall) and the chassis frame. On the Willys bodies they are flat with five holes; on the Ford bodies they have rounded corners and have just three holes. On the later composite bodies, the Ford design with three holes was retained. There are also some differences between Willys and Ford bodies in the way the cowl is formed; again, the Ford style prevailed after the switch to composite bodies. The Ford rear wheelarch has two vertical stiffening swages in its side, and another on the top behind the locker lid, but these are not present on Willys bodies.

The Jeep body tub has no doors, but only cutouts in the body sides. These were designed to make rapid entry and exit as easy as possible, but in some circumstances – such as when driving over rough terrain – they were just as likely to make it easy for the front seat occupants to fall out of the vehicle. So a safety-strap arrangement was devised. The rear end of the strap was bolted to the inside of the body tub behind the aperture, and the front end had a cast latch which hooked onto an eye-bolt screwed into the bulkhead (firewall) on each side. From approximately January 1944, Ford Jeeps came with stamped steel hooks instead of the cast type.

BODY & FITTINGS

Some of the "poppers" for fixing the canvas half-door can be seen around the door opening here….

… and in this picture the canvas half-door is in place.

Half-doors

All Jeeps were built with a set of seven receiver sockets around each door aperture, to take the studs of a canvas half-door. These sockets are sometimes missing and some owners have even welded the holes up during restoration, but their total absence is a sure sign of a reproduction body tub. The sockets are a press-fit and expand to grip behind the metal when correctly "set".

The half-doors themselves are made of canvas, shaped to fit the aperture, and have an edge binding. They were made by several different suppliers and their colour – always supposedly Olive Drab – very often does not match the canvas roof very well. The doors are only rarely seen today, for several reasons. One is that the canvas can shrink, which makes them impossible to fit. Another is that supplies seem to have dried up during 1944 and that the final Jeeps did not have them (although they did have the fixing sockets).

Body serial number

All Willys and composite bodies have a six-digit serial number, but the bodies built by Ford have no such number. Note that the body serial number, where present, does not match either the chassis frame serial number or the engine serial number. It is therefore really of academic interest only.

When a body serial number is present, it is stamped into the driver's side toeboard gusset, which runs between the lower bulkhead (firewall) and the chassis frame on the engine side.

The front end of the safety strap and the receiver loop on the bulkhead are seen here on a 1945 Jeep.

FITTINGS

Body mountings

The body tub is bolted to the chassis at 16 points. In the beginning, rubber mounting washers were used to insulate one from the other, but when rubber became in demand during 1942 as US involvement in the war increased, these were replaced by the fabric shims which will be found on the majority of wartime Jeeps. These fabric shims were glued in place during manufacture.

Very early Willys models have flat washers between the rear body panel and the frame, but these were replaced on production in January 1942 (at MB 111247) by a plain type. There are eight of these washers on later models.

23

The lifting handles were bolted to either side of the body and to the rear corners. These are pictured on a 1945 model.

Ford made sure their branding was everywhere they could put it. This is the script "F" on the securing bolts of a lifting handle on a 1945 Jeep.

Lifting handles

Every Jeep has four lifting handles bolted to the body tub, and their purpose is to make it easier for soldiers to physically lift a stranded vehicle out of a ditch or from some other predicament.

There is one handle on each side just ahead of the rear wheel arch, and a second that wraps around the rear corner of the body. There are minor differences between the Willys and Ford handles, although the most obvious one is that the Ford handles are branded with a script "F" on one of the flanges by which they are attached.

Rear panel

From the start of slat-grille production in October 1941, Willys stamped its name prominently into the left-hand side of the rear body panel, just inboard of the tail light. Not to be outdone, Ford did the same when it began producing its own bodies, using the familiar Ford script logo. However, from approximately July 1942, this practice was discontinued on the instructions of the Quartermaster Corps. These early body tubs are usually described as "script" types now. Exact figures are not available, but at a rough estimate there were approximately 47,000 Willys "script" Jeeps, and 50,000 Ford "script" Jeeps.

The handles on the rear corners also gave a certain amount of protection to the body, although the dents in the picture above show that they were not always successful.

A "script" body: the Willys name was pressed into the tail panel of the Jeeps manufactured by that company until the US Government forbade it in summer 1942.

BODY & FITTINGS

The rear panel itself then remained unchanged, although there were still differences between the Willys and Ford types. There is a top-hat section behind the tail light aperture for mounting the light unit, and on the Willys bodies this is mounted horizontally; the Ford type is mounted vertically; and of course the composite bodies all have the Willys pattern.

There were multiple changes to the items mounted on that rear panel. From October 1942, the panel itself was reinforced around the mounting for the spare wheel carrier (see below) on both Willys and Ford bodies, because vibration of the heavy spare wheel had caused breakages. Worth noting, too, is that at MB 200741 in January 1943, a pair of reinforcing brackets were added to the inside of the panel, in each case alongside the tool locker on the relevant side. These brackets were not used on MZ-1 radio Jeeps for the US Marine Corps because they compromised the space available for the radio itself, and the Marine Corps Jeeps did not get them until late in 1944.

Spare wheel support bracket

The Jeep's spare wheel was always mounted to a bracket that was bolted at four points to the rear panel. On early models, the wheel was simply suspended in mid-air, but from October 1943 an additional support bracket or foot was bolted to the rear panel, underneath the wheel, to prevent the panel from cracking.

Both Willys and Ford bodies used three-stud carriers in the beginning, but a stronger two-stud carrier was standardised during August 1943; on Willys production, this occurred at approximately MB 26000, but the change may not have taken place on the bodies that Ford used until the Type 2 or composite bodies began to reach assembly lines around December 1943.

With this three-stud carrier came the additional support bracket already mentioned, and a wheel retaining disc. Inevitably, the Willys and Ford retaining discs were different: the Willys item had only two holes, for the wheel retaining studs to pass through, and the Ford version had two smaller holes aligned vertically between them.

Jerrycan support bracket

From August 1942, a square plate was spot-welded to the outside of the rear panel on the left-hand side, above the tail light and just inboard of it. This was intended to reinforce the panel when a spare fuel can was carried, although in the beginning the jerrycan and its support bracket had to be ordered from the Ordnance Department separately by user units and had to be fitted in the field.

The plate became standard on Willys production at MB 166582, and was added to Ford bodies at about the same time. However, the support bracket did not become a standard factory-fit item until March 1943 and Willys MB 217309; once again, the move was parallelled on Ford production but the exact changeover point is not known.

The support bracket (or jerrycan holder) was bolted to the rear panel and had two securing straps made of webbing for the jerrycan itself. These straps were attached with brass rivets and were supplied from various different sources; as a result there are minor differences among straps. For details of the jerrycan, see Section 5, under Fuel System.

Rear foot rest

There is a foot rest mounted on each side of the rear floor behind the front seats. The Willys type has a tube held between two brackets, one of which is bolted to floor and the other to the body side. The Ford type, typically simpler, has a triangular floor end bracket that is welded to the tube. Some of the Ford brackets have a cutout in the floor end bracket.

Tool boxes

All Jeep bodies have a tool box behind each rear wheelarch, and there are differences between the Willys and Ford types.

Each tool box has a hinged lid, and this lid can be held closed by a catch. A locking button located on the inward face of the locker releases this catch, and each locking button incorporates a keylock. On Ford bodies, there is a rectangular depression around the locking button, but on the Willys bodies and on the 1944 and later composite bodies (which used the Willys design of rear body) the depression is circular.

There is a further difference in the tool box lids. The Willys tool box lid is a plain flat type, but the Ford design has a stiffening "frame" pressed into the metal and a circular feature in the centre. On the Willys lids, the hinge is held in place with individual nuts and bolts; on the Ford lids, the nuts are brazed onto a metal strip. Slat-grille models each had a pair of small hinges, but from MB 118600 in February 1942 both Willys

This rear view of a 1942 model shows the jerrycan and its webbing securing strap; a securing strap for the hood sticks; and the retaining disc for the spare wheel. This is actually an early Ford GPW and would have had the retaining disc with two extra holes when new.

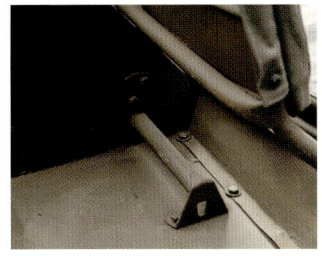

This is the Ford type of foot rest, with a triangular support welded to the inboard end.

The tool box lids in the Willys MB were always flat.....

... and were quite different from the distinctively pressed shape of the Ford tool box lid.

This 1945 Ford GPW has a composite body. The circular depression around the tool box release was a Willys feature that was carried over.

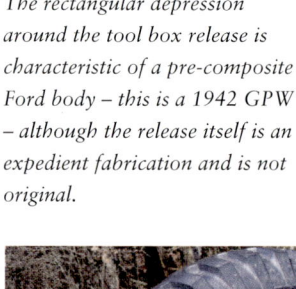

The rectangular depression around the tool box release is characteristic of a pre-composite Ford body – this is a 1942 GPW – although the release itself is an expedient fabrication and is not original.

and Ford-built Jeeps had a single longer piano-type hinge.

Note that each manufacturer continued to use its own design of tool box lid (and other bolt-on parts as well) after the composite bodies were introduced. So the plain flat tool box lid remained associated with the Willys MB and the embossed lid remained associated with the Ford GPW, despite the fact that both used the same basic composite body.

Early tool box lids have rubber seals, but in pursuit of the military policy to reduce rubber in the vehicles, both manufacturers made changes over the summer and autumn of 1942. In July that year, at MB 156083, Willys changed to a jute seal; Ford complied a little later, switching to a cork seal possibly some time after November 1942.

The tyre pump was stowed under the rear seat, and the owner of this Jeep has also taken the precaution of including a towbar for emergencies! On the left can be seen the flat tool locker lid of a Willys-built Jeep, this one dating from 1943.

BODY & FITTINGS

The starting-handle can just be seen here, held to the rear panel in clips and tucked out of the way behind the rear seat.

Minor differences: the damper cover on the right-hand side of this 1945 Jeep has a straight front face, but.....

..... its equivalent on the left-hand side has an angled face. Also clear here is the Willys type of foot rest, with a separate hooped bracket over its inboard end.

The "wing" mirror was bolted to a bracket that in turn was bolted to the side of the cowl.

Wing mirror

Strictly speaking, the wing mirror is not a wing mirror at all, because it is attached to the cowl and not to the wing. The attachment depends on a swivel bracket that is bolted in place on the driver's side. There is then a tubular arm with an adjusting nut and a circular mirror head at the top.

The mirror normally had a plain steel backing with a lip around its outer edge, and a central bolt that passed through the top of the arm. Mirrors were made by King Bee and were common to several other US military vehicles of the period. They have blue-tinted glass, and the steel body of at least some of those used on Ford production was marked with the F script. Mirror bodies were painted to match the Jeep's bodywork.

The Willys and Ford mirror mounting arms have differences. Early Willys arms have a squarish collar with a hex head adjusting bolt, but later changed to a rounded collar with a square-headed adjusting nut. Ford arms always had the rounded collar and square-headed nut. They were also marked with the F script identification, and most had a drain hole at the bottom that was not present on the equivalent Willys item. Some early Ford arms are thought to have had a more complex design with a hexagonal locking nut near the top.

There was a support bracket for the hood bows on either side of the rear tub, securely bolted in place. This one is on a 1945 Ford GPW, and displays the ubiquitous script "F".

This curved section of the rear floor covered the weapons mount on the chassis frame below.

27

FACTORY-ORIGINAL WARTIME JEEPS

The slat-grille was used on the first 25,000 MB Jeeps.

A rare feature, fitted to Jeeps supplied to the Canadian army, was this headlamp guard. The example shown is probably a reproduction item.

The pressed grille was simpler to manufacture and took over during 1942. It lasted until the end of production and is seen here on a 1945 model.

Front wings (fenders)

The front wings (fenders) are simple pressings, with an additional lower projection that runs low down ahead of the "door" aperture. They are bolted to the main body tub and the lower section is bolted to the chassis frame.

Grille

The change from a "slat" grille to a "pressed" type is one of the most well-known of all the alterations made to the wartime Jeep during production.

The Willys MB entered production with the "slat" grille, which was welded together from flat iron bars. There were 12 vertical slats plus shaped sections around the headlights, and making this grille was clearly a quite labour-intensive operation. Nevertheless, it was fitted to the first 25,000 Jeeps that Willys built in 1941-1942.

There were only minor variations. These original grilles incorporated a deflector on either side to channel air towards the radiator, and in the beginning each deflector was a two-piece assembly. However, from MB 108452 in January 1942, Willys fitted redesigned deflectors which were single-piece assemblies. Another variation was seen on the Jeeps built under a Canadian Army contract during February 1942, which had simple headlamp guards welded to the grille slats and top bar. These were essentially two flat strips of metal bent to fit and welded together to form a visor-like structure over the top half of each headlamp.

Ford's greater production engineering expertise led that company to redesign the grille from the start. Their grille was created by a single pressing operation on a flat piece of metal, which punched holes for the headlights and the blackout marker lights below them, and nine vertical slots to allow air through. There was no provision for any air deflectors, and

BODY & FITTINGS

Webbing acted as a buffer to prevent the bonnet fretting against the grille panel, and was riveted in place.

The bonnet was held closed by a sprung latch attached to each front wing. A similar latch attached to the bonnet on each side normally rested in a keep and was intended to secure the windscreen when this was folded forwards onto the bonnet.

indeed none were needed. The Ford grille was lighter than the Willys type, cheaper to make, and obviously much less labour-intensive. So all the Ford GPW models had this type of grille from the start of their production in January 1942.

The logic of the Ford design was immediately clear. So during March 1942, beginning at chassis number MB 125809, Willys adopted the Ford type of pressed grille as well, and it continued unchanged on both Willys and Ford Jeeps until the end of wartime production. Ironically, perhaps, the Ford-designed vertical-slat grille is now a signature feature of modern Jeep products, which are built by a company that is descended from Willys-Overland.

Bonnet (hood) panel

There were several differences between Willys and Ford bonnets (hoods), and these panels also evolved during wartime production to incorporate changes.

There are differences in the hinge, which on the slat-grille Willys has nine segments as against the 11 segments on later panels. Ford items have a script F stamped on the hinge between the bolt holes. Ford bonnets also had tooling imprints – rather like the serrations on the edge of a coin – on the underside of the rolled-over edge at the front of the bonnet. The Willys bonnet panels did not. However, this is not an infallible guide because the tooling marks on a Ford bonnet may have been lost over the years by over-enthusiastic flatting down during restoration, or they may simply be invisible under several layers of paint.

Buffers were mounted on the bonnet for the folded windscreen. Early support blocks were made of rubber but from 1942 the buffers were made of hardwood with a webbing strip screwed in place as the buffering medium.

The four bolt-heads visible on the bonnet side here indicate that this 1945 model has a grease gun bracket mounted on the inside of the bonnet. This is a Ford-built Jeep and therefore has pan-head bolts. Two of the four securing bolts for the lubrication chart holder can also be seen here, on the flat section of the panel.

Near the rear of the Willys bonnet, a top-hat reinforcing section allowed more effective drainage, but early Ford GPW bonnets did not have this. The Willys bonnet also has an air deflector on its underside, but the Ford bonnet does not. Nevertheless, when Ford were using bodies from Willys' supplier ACM, they used them complete with that air deflector.

During 1943, the QMC compared examples of the Willys MB and Ford GPW to check that minor changes to the original design introduced by each company had not compromised the plan for standardisation. The Ford bonnet is said to have turned out to be not as rigid as the Willys type, although there is no indication that any changes were made as a result of this discovery.

Hood blocks

Two bonnet blocks (hood blocks) were attached to the forward outer ends of the bonnet panel to prevent it from damaging the windscreen when opened right back. There were at least three different types of these, and both research and controversy continue.

The earliest ones were made of dark green rubber and had a channel running down the middle. Willys changed to a black rubber block with a domed top and no channel from MB 125809 in March 1942, and this lasted until the rubber shortage forced a change in autumn 1942. Ford meanwhile stayed with the green rubber type.

The autumn 1942 replacements from Willys and Ford differed. At MB 163750 Willys introduced a hardwood block with slightly chamfered top edges, but Ford used a hardwood block with a channel in the top and a webbing insert that acted as a buffer. Wood and webbing were always coloured Olive Drab. The Willys wooden blocks tended to crack and split, and eventually to fall off, and so from MB 218344 in March 1943 Willys adopted the Ford style of block.

The next change occurred in March 1945, when the driver's side block (but not the one on the passenger's side) was relocated about 1.5in further forwards so that it would not foul the wiper arm of the new vacuum wiper system when the bonnet was fully opened and leant against the screen.

Under-hood fittings

Later Jeeps had two additional fittings under the bonnet (hood), although there is still some disagreement about when these became standard. One was a grease gun holder, and the other a lubrication chart holder.

During December 1943, a mounting bracket for the grease gun was added under the bonnet, on the vertical side section on the driver's side. The bonnet itself had a reinforcing plate spot-welded in place before being drilled for four fixings to suit the bracket. The bracket was secured by round-headed bolts on Willys Jeeps and by pan-head bolts on Ford types. There are details of the grease gun itself in Section 7 on Additions.

A Technical Bulletin from March 1944 makes clear that a lubrication chart had been drawn up for the Jeep, and supplies of these charts began to reach the assembly plants probably a couple of months later. The chart was to be kept in a metal "pocket" that was attached under the bonnet near the centre-line on the driver's side, and bonnets were pre-drilled with four holes to allow this to be bolted in place.

It is generally accepted that these chart holders began to be fitted around July 1944, although John Farley puts the date much later, at December 1944. The chart holder often (but perhaps not invariably) had "Lubrication Order" stencilled on it in white. Each holder also had a pair of rubber buffers near the bottom, on which the chart could be propped while maintenance work was being done on the vehicle.

The lubrication chart itself changed in spring 1945 to a

There is no agreement about when the underbonnet holders for the grease gun and lubrication chart were introduced, but they were certainly in place by the time of this 1945 model. The two rubber buffers against which the chart could be propped are visible inboard of the lower securing nuts in this picture.

The lubrication chart was War Department publication number 501 and was mounted in a metal frame. The charts carried a date of issue in the bottom right-hand corner: this one was issued on 25 April 1944,

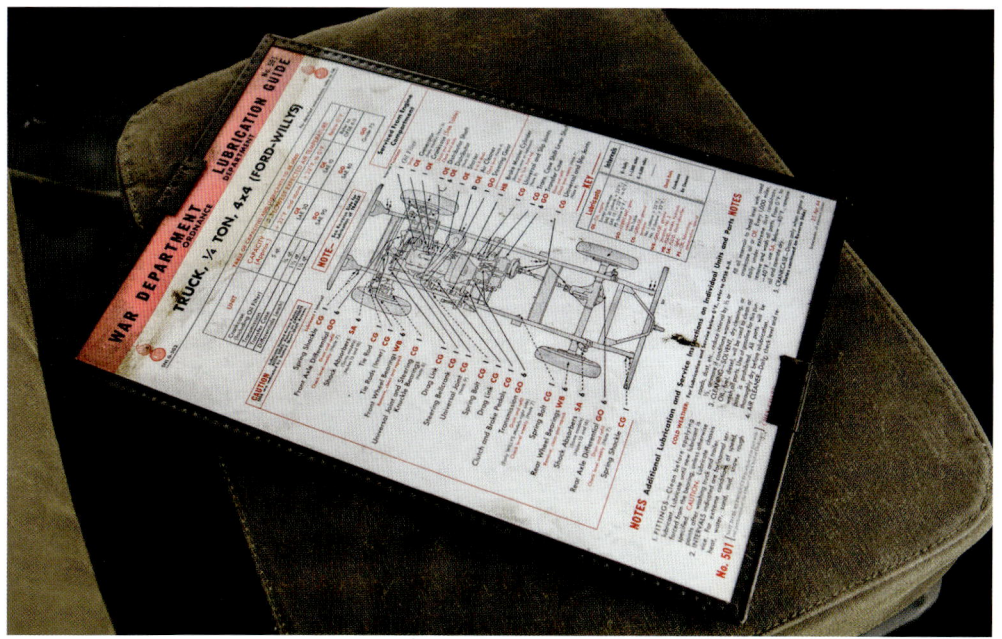

larger one that is generally called the "tri-fold" type. This was not intended to be kept in the under-bonnet chart holder (it was probably more commonly kept in the glove box), which therefore became redundant. John Farley notes that several Willys MBs built from April 1945 seem not to have had the chart holder, but it seems clear that Ford continued to fit the chart holder for rather longer, perhaps into the early summer of 1945. Perhaps the reason was that the Ford assembly plants had greater stocks of pre-drilled bonnets to use up than the Willys plant did.

The windscreen assembly is seen here on a 1942 Ford GPW, with the early bolted handle on the lower frame rail. The rear-view mirror is a modern addition, but a sensible one.

All windscreens had two panes of glass. The top rail carried fasteners to secure the canvas top. Also clear in this picture is the rubber seal around the opening section of the assembly.

BODY & FITTINGS

The whole windscreen assembly could be folded forward onto the bonnet. The pivots were tightened by a wing nut, which on this 1945 example has been wired to prevent theft.

Windscreen (windshield)

The windscreen (windshield) consists of a metal frame containing two separate panes of glass, and the whole assembly is mounted on curved arms attached to the scuttle so that it can be folded flat onto the bonnet after loosening a pair of wing nuts. When folded in this way, it can be secured in place by latches. When erect, it is secured in position by a pair of catches on the dash panel. On early models these were cast from bronze, but between the summer and autumn of 1942 a pressed steel type became standard. No precise changeover points are known, but Ford are thought to have made the change in mid-1942, possibly slightly before Willys did so in approximately September 1942. The catches were always painted to match the vehicle body.

The earliest Willys MB models were built with the windscreen assembly from the MA, which had a noticeably shallower metal panel below the glass than the later standard production type. In December 1941, at MB 103545, the standard production type was introduced, with the deeper metal panel and drain holes near the bottom outer edges. The positions of the windscreen latches and their retainers were changed to suit the new screen assembly.

The standard windscreen assembly consists of inner and outer frames. The inner frame carries the glass, an inner rubber

The windscreen assembly was secured in the erect position by a pair of over-centre catches like this one. Also visible here is the rubber buffer between the frame and the bulkhead.

weather seal, and adjustable arms which allow the angle of the screen to be altered. A grab handle on the inside at the bottom of this inner frame aids screen adjustment; on early models this is bolted in place but on later ones it is welded. The outer frame has a rubber seal between the bottom of the windscreen

33

This was what the gun holder looked like, and this one is pictured with a (deactivated) US M1 Garand rifle. One of the adjustable windscreen arms can also be seen, with its locking turnwheel clearly visible.

Mounting brackets for the gun holder were welded to the lower section of the windscreen frame.

assembly and the cowl, and this seal was not painted on production. The two panes of glass are marked Willys or Ford, according to the manufacturer of that assembly, and are made of ¼-inch thick laminated glass.

The top rail of the outer frame also carries a series of fastening studs for the canvas top. On early windscreen assemblies, these fasteners have a narrow solid top and a threaded bolt that passes into the windscreen frame. However, from August 1942 (at MB 164554) the ferrule was changed to a design with a capstan shape and recessed top, and was retained by a cadmium-plated screw that goes into the windscreen frame. These later fixings were made by the Cinch Manufacturing Company in Chicago, and the ferrule was either parkerised or cadmium plated before being finished in Olive Drab.

A rifle holder on the inside of the metal windscreen panel became part of the standard specification in September 1943 (the first Willys with it was MB 261578, but there were different start points at the different Ford assembly plants). Its introduction was simply an acknowledgement that units in the field had been adding their own rifle holders for some time. From July 1942, for example, Jeeps used by the British armed forces could be fitted with two brackets on the windscreen panel to hold a rifle.

The factory-installed rifle holder was mounted to the lower windscreen panel by two brackets, and was painted Olive Drab. By June 1944 it was being fitted with a U-shaped clip to suit a Thompson sub-machine gun instead of a standard rifle.

BODY & FITTINGS

The early type of windscreen rail fastenings for the canvas top had solid ends. They are seen here on a slat-grille model.

Viewed from the outside, this is one of the adjustable arms for the glass section of the windscreen. The locking turnwheel was always on the inside face of the arm.

Windscreen wipers

The windscreen wipers were always mounted at the top of the windscreen frame and were initially operated by a crude manual system. This was needed because the windscreen was removable, and otherwise complicated electrical connections would have been necessary.

On the earliest models, each wiper was individually operated by a hand crank on the inside of the windscreen assembly. However, a tandem system with a linking rod was introduced during August 1943 on both Ford and Willys models. The two wipers were linked on the inside of the windscreen frame by a bar running between them, and there was again a hand crank for each one, so that either the driver or the front-seat passenger could operate the system.

The Jeeps delivered to the Canadian Army from February 1942, and those for the US Marine Corps and the US Navy, had an electric wiper system for the driver's side only, with a motor manufactured by Owens-Dyneto and a suppression filter mounted on the motor. The body of this motor was probably black when delivered to the assembly lines but was painted to match the vehicle's body during assembly. The passenger's side wiper on Jeeps with this system remained hand-operated.

A vacuum operated wiper system was introduced late in production, operated by manifold depression. The exact start number for the Willys MB is not known, but the first Ford to have it is thought to have been serial number 269248. This was assembled in early May 1945, and the change was probably introduced on the MB at about the same time. The vehicles were prepared for its introduction by the addition of a hole in the cowl for the vacuum hose.

The vacuum "motor unit" for each wiper was a Trico S-583-1 type, and was mounted to the windscreen top rail on the inside. These units had a half-moon shape and there is still some controversy about which way up they were mounted. The

Crude but (just about) effective: the windscreen wipers were operated manually by a crank handle.

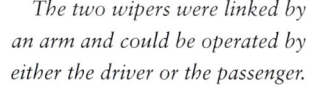

The two wipers were linked by an arm and could be operated by either the driver or the passenger.

Two receiver catches like this were screwed to the top rail of the windscreen and engaged with the sprung latches on the bonnet when the screen assembly was folded flat.

vacuum part of the system began with a copper pipe tapped into the inlet manifold, which was then connected to a black rubber hose that ran through a hole in the cowl. The next element was a copper pipe running up the driver's side of the windscreen frame, where it was attached by plated clips. This then fed into a Y-piece from which one rubber hose went to the driver's side motor unit and the other to a copper pipe running across the windscreen top rail; a short rubber hose then made the final connection between this and the passenger's side wiper unit.

The wiper blades were very simple straight types with a 9.5in length. They were made of black rubber and permanently held in metal frames. Each frame was then clipped to its operating arm. All metal parts of the wiper and arm were painted to match the vehicle's body.

The late type of vacuum-operated wipers can be seen here, where they have been fitted retrospectively to a 1942 model. There is still some controversy about the correct "plumbing" for the vacuum pipes, and indeed about which way up the half-moon wiper units were originally mounted.

Bonnet and windscreen latches

At the forward end of each front wing (fender) is mounted an anchor-like sprung latch. This engages with a receiver on the bonnet itself and is designed to ensure that the bonnet remains securely closed. On the bonnet is a second sprung latch, mounted close to the receiver of the bonnet latch and normally retained by a "keep" on the bonnet. All these latches, receivers and keeps were painted to match the body.

Dealing first with the bonnet latches, these should have a D-shaped stem; the curved surface should face outwards and the flat side of the stem should lie against the bonnet. Bonnet latches that have round stems are post-war types. There are some minor variations in these latches, which probably came about because more than one supplier was used. However, the subject is still under research. The stems have holes in different positions, and there are differences where the stem joins the T-handle: some are flat but others have a small indent at the join.

The pressing in the base-plate through which each latch passes is not central but is located to one side of the plate. It is possible to mount them the wrong way round, but the correct mounting allows the latch to fall away from the side of the bonnet when unlatched, so that it is impossible to close the bonnet on the latch itself.

The windscreen latches are different, with an L-shaped lower end where they pass through the mounting plate. Once again the stem is D-shaped with a flat underside, and there is a hole in the stem as well. Post-war equivalents have round stems. On the first Willys Jeeps, these catches were mounted to the bonnet just behind the receiver for the bonnet latch, and hung diagonally downwards when hooked into their own "keep". This arrangement suited the early MA-type windscreen. However, when the taller MB windscreen became available in December 1941, the latches were repositioned to suit. Their new position was just above the receiver for the bonnet latch, and the keep was relocated level with this and nearer the bulkhead (firewall). This became the definitive arrangement.

There are unproven suggestions that the latches were all made stronger from April 1942. What certainly did happen at about this time was that Willys adopted the Ford type of bonnet latch retainer, which looks generally more roughly cast than the original Willys type.

As a factory fit, there were only ever these four latches. Nevertheless, some units in the field added extra catches to hold the bonnet (hood) more firmly in place. A known example was in Italy, where one unit added extra latches to the rear of the bonnet panel to reduce strain on the bonnet hinges from use over rough mountain roads.

Canvas top

The canvas top was never intended to provide more than basic weather-proofing, and consisted of a single assembly that formed a roof and a rear upright section with a window aperture. Various additional pieces of canvas were sometimes added in the field to give better weather protection, but as often as not a Jeep would be used without the canvas in place. In those circumstances, the canvas would be stowed under the front passenger seat. Two single straps and four footman loops attached to the crossbars of the seat were used to hold the folded top in place.

There were two basic types of canvas roof, the first one used until spring 1942 and the second one thereafter. Both are made from military-grade canvas and feature edge binding and heavy-duty webbing. Hardware of eyelets, fasteners, buckles and strap ends (tips) was always finished in black.

On the early type, the rear window aperture is oblong with rounded corners and is reinforced down each edge. The rear panel has six straps, and the top panel has three double canvas flaps which attached to the folding bow. There are ten eyelets to hold the front of the canvas top to the top rail of the windscreen. On the later type, the differences lie in the number of rear straps – five instead of six – and in the provision of a rectangular hole which allows the jerrycan strap to pass through the canvas. In both cases, the canvas was US military type number 8, in Olive Drab.

The canvas top afforded only minimum protection from the elements when erected.

A full set of sidescreens was available but the difficulty of attaching them satisfactorily means they are rarely seen!

Winter enclosure kit

A winter kit that provided full sidescreens for the Jeep was available. This is variously described as a winter canvas set and a body enclosure field kit, and genuine examples are rare.

The kit consisted of a special canvas top with attachment points along its sides from which the side curtains could be hung. The two side curtains themselves were the only other elements of the kit. When erected and attached to the body, they provided a weatherproof enclosure with celluloid windows and a flap for hand signals on the driver's side.

It is likely that there was more than one design of this kit. However, as a word of warning, it appears that some Jeeps that served the military of other countries after the 1939-1945 war were fitted with similar kits of local manufacture. There were also several quite professional looking sets of sidescreens that were made up by units in the field.

Roof bows

When erected, the roof was held in place by tubular bows (sometimes called hood sticks) which were pivoted from sockets mounted on the rear sides of the Jeep. These provided the necessary height; the canvas was attached to the rear of the vehicle by webbing straps and to the top rail of the windscreen by holes which hooked over ferrules.

The two roof bows fold together flat and can be detached from their mounting on the body side for stowage along the top of the rear tub. There are two clamps on each side of the body to hold the stowed roof bows in place, and there are minor differences between the Willys and Ford types of clamp: most obviously, the Willys type has an extra hole in its turned-over end, and the Ford type is branded with a script F. The first few Ford GPW models used hood bows made by Willys, but Ford had its own bows in production by February 1942.

The bow sockets on the rear sides of the body tub are held in place by three fixings – two screws and one bolt. The Ford version carries an F script marking. A safety chain attached to the socket prevents the bows from jumping out of engagement with it.

Paint

Jeeps were generally given an initial coat of red oxide primer before the top coat of paint was applied. It is probable (but not proven) that all Jeeps were initially painted Olive Drab, and that when another colour was required it was painted over this. Most vehicles retained their Olive Drab colour in service, but those used by the US Marine Corps appear to have been painted Marine Corps Green and many (possibly all) of those used by the US Navy were painted Navy Gray.

Olive Drab was known to the Quartermaster Corps as Color no 22. There were minor changes to the formulation of the paint during the war as such things as pigment shortages affected production. The Jeeps for the US Navy all came from

BODY & FITTINGS

With canvas erect, the rear of the vehicle always presented a curious and distinctive profile.

As all Jeeps had left-hand drive, this warning was a sensible precaution on those used in Britain at a time when hand signals were the norm to indicate an intention to turn.

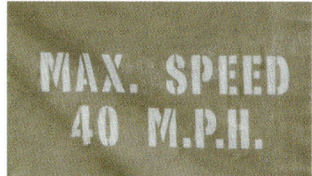

Not so much a legal requirement as a warning to traffic following behind....

a single batch of 653 vehicles built by Ford under a specific contract in 1942; John Farley adds that a further 9 were subsequently built for the Navy.

Standard markings

The issue of Jeep markings is one that could fill a book on its own, so this book gives only an overview of the markings that were applied at the factory. All sorts of other markings were applied by units to vehicles in service.

From the start of Jeep production until February 1945, US Army regulations called for markings to be made in Blue Drab. This colour was chosen because it was difficult to distinguish from the background Olive Drab in a black-and-white photograph – so hindering enemy intelligence gathering.

In February 1945, the regulations changed to call for flat white marking, but in practice supplies of Blue Drab continued to be used until they ran out. When vehicles were repainted in the field, they often received white numbers of varying sizes and in fonts different from the regulation type: expediency ruled.

US Army Jeeps had the military identification number stencilled on each side of the bonnet (hood). The number invariably began with 20 (the code denoting a reconnaissance vehicle), and this was followed by a five-digit serial number –

39

The canvas can be stored temporarily at the rear, attached to the bows, as here, but is more commonly removed altogether. The screw clamp for the bows has been wired here, to prevent theft.

When the Jeep is used in open mode, the hood bows are stored on the top surfaces of the body tub.

Canvas of a different kind.... this slat-grille model is fitted with a canvas map pocket that attaches to the bonnet.

or, on later Jeeps, a six-digit number. Above the serial number was the legend "U.S.A." (complete with stops after each letter). Regulations required all numbers and letters to be two inches high. On those Jeeps which had suppression equipment (to suit a military radio), the letter S was added as a suffix to the military identification number, preceded by a dash and painted in the same colour.

From July 1942, all Jeeps passed through the US military before allocation to US forces or to Allied forces. As a result, they were all stencilled with a US registration number at the factory before delivery. So on a Jeep used by British forces, it is quite possible to find the US registration number on the lower bonnet sides (often under layers of Olive Drab) while the British registration number is in white letters slightly higher up on the flat surface.

British markings are another big subject that cannot be covered in detail here. However, British registration numbers began with an M, which was followed by seven numbers; there is more about them in the Appendix.

One other set of numbers was used on some Jeeps, probably beginning in mid-1942. This appears to have been associated with USAAF vehicles that were used in Britain, and consists of an X prefix with a five-number registration.

Jeeps which spent time in Britain before D-Day typically had a white stencilled warning on the rear of the canvas top, which read: "Caution left-hand drive/ No Signal". This was intended to alert following drivers to the fact that they could not expect the hand signals that British drivers normally used to indicate an intention to turn or slow down.

Note that tyre pressures were not marked on wings above the wheels; this was a practice that began after the war was over. However, a marking such as TP35 was sometimes painted on the dashboard, inside the windscreen glass, or inside the wheel wells. The example here would indicate that Tyre Pressures were to be 35psi all round.

This picture shows the way the pioneer tools looked before receiving their coat of body-coloured paint.

Pioneer tools

The left-hand side of the Jeep body tub has a pair of indentations which are designed to accommodate the handles of pioneer tools. The tools are secured in place by brackets, and the Willys and Ford versions of these differ. The Ford brackets are readily recognisable from their script F marking.

The tools normally consisted of a spade and an axe. The axe was a standard US military issue 2.5kg type with a wooden handle, and the spade was a "no 2" type, again to standard military specification and with a wooden handle. The US-issue spades came with a D-handle, and from around August 1944 a second type was introduced, with a recess in the back where the handle fitted.

The tools were normally painted in Olive Drab – although the paint soon came off their business ends when the tools were used in anger.

The axe is painted here, but the spade is not. More importantly, this picture shows the fixing arrangements for the pioneer tools, with metal brackets at the front end and webbing straps through brackets at the rear.

The indentations in the body side are easy to see on this 1945 model. Spade and axe are painted to match the bodywork, as they typically would have been – but have clearly not seen much use!

LIGHTING & ELECTRICS

A 6-volt electrical system with negative earth was standard on US military vehicles at the time of the Jeep's conception, and the vehicle was drawn up to use a number of standard military parts. The aim of this was to simplify workshop logistics. Examples of the standard electrical components were the 5-inch sealed-beam headlamps and the black-out lamps that were fitted front and rear. Note that a good number of preserved Jeeps have been converted to more modern 12-volt electrics, often using components that were introduced for the post-war CJ-2A civilian models derived from the MB. The conversion to 12-volt electrics requires several changes in electrical equipment – and for safety should always be accompanied by renewal of old wiring.

WIRING HARNESS & CIRCUIT BREAKERS

The standard wiring harness on Willys Jeeps has a black woven cotton cover. By contrast, Ford harnesses were plastic-wrapped. Some elements of both harnesses were wrapped in metal braid. Good quality replacements of both types are available from specialists, as are reproductions of the original junction blocks.

Jeeps were never fitted with fuses. Instead, they had circuit-breakers which would trip and then re-set, so removing the immediate cause of danger and allowing time for it to be investigated. There are three circuit-breakers in all, two of them mounted on a brace that runs between the bulkhead (firewall) and the centre of the dash, and the third one built into the main lighting switch. These circuit breakers were originally manufactured by FA Smith or Klixon; the Smith ones had a black bakelite body and the Klixon ones had a metal body.

The two mounted behind the centre of the dash were originally a 5 amp type for the fuel gauge and a 15 amp type for the horn (note that the horn is always live, and operates when it is earthed by pushing the horn button). Later in production, the 5-amp circuit breaker was replaced by a second 15-amp type. Both types of main lighting switch – push-pull and rotary – have a thermal circuit breaker.

CHARGING SYSTEM

The electrical system on all Jeeps is conventional, with a storage battery that is kept charged by an engine-driven generator and a voltage regulator to keep the charging system in check.

Battery

The 6-volt battery is always located on the passenger's side at the front of the engine bay. Original batteries were always black with a hard rubber casing, and were 10in long, 7in wide and 8 5/16in tall; they are held in position by a metal battery clamp with triangular corners. This clamp was always painted Olive Drab on Ford models; on Willys models, some clamps were Olive Drab and some were gloss black. When a 12-volt conversion is made, space has to be made for the physically larger battery, and this can involve moving some original components.

The battery cable terminals have screw-type clamps, which have "P" and "+" or "N" and "–" cast into them to aid identification. The earth cable from the battery is always a round type with a black plastic sheath, and on early Jeeps runs to an earthing point on the front cross-member. It was probably some time early in 1944 that the change was made to a shorter cable which earthed to a bolt on the battery tray.

Generator

The generator (dynamo) is a standard 40-amp QMC (Quartermaster Corps) type, as used on several US Army trucks of the period. Willys MB models always had an Autolite generator. Ford production started with the Autolite type but during June 1942 changed to a Ford-made generator. This was used until late 1942 or early 1943, when Ford reverted to the Autolite type. All generators had a Satin Black finish.

The early Autolite generator has part number GEG5001A. In late February or March 1942, a GEG5002D generator became standard in its place. Generators normally had a capacitor mounted to them, but parts shortages in late 1941 meant that this was omitted from Jeeps numbered MB103001 to MB112925, beginning in December 1941.

Voltage regulator

Autolite also manufactured the voltage regulator, which is mounted on the right-hand (passenger's side) inner front wing.

There were two standard varieties of regulator, each one identified by a part number on a metal tag on the cover. (Note that there was also a special type for vehicles converted to 12 volts for radio use; see Appendix.) The early type is

The early type of regulator box has a smooth cover. All original regulators had a small plate identifying badge on that cover, and that plate can also be seen here. The battery terminal clamps are not the original type, but the six-volt battery is held in place by the correct type of frame clamp with triangular corners.

All regulator boxes had a crackle-black finish. This is the later type, identifiable by ribbing on its cover, and is pictured on a 1945 GPW.

VRY4203A, which has a smooth cover finished in crackle-black paint and a cork seal between the cover and the base. It has a plated identification tag on its cover, which is etched aluminium with a red and orange background. At MB 112925 during January 1942, a filter was added to the voltage regulator. These filters were made by both Sprague and the Tobe Deutschmann Corporation.

The second type of regulator was introduced in March or April 1944 and was numbered VRY4203G. This had a ribbed cover, again finished in crackle-black paint, and after January 1945 came with a rubber seal between the cover and the base. Some experts have suggested that other varieties of voltage regulator also came into the picture. Those suggested include a VRY4203B (from January 1944 to October 1944 on Willys, but possibly not on Fords) and a VRY4203D (with ribbed casing and cork gasket, from August 1943). The filter on late Ford models was made by PR Mallory & Co, Inc, and carried Ford markings.

These regulators could be troublesome, and it is now possible to replace their internals with an electronic conversion kit that remains invisible from the outside and provides modern reliability. The regulator is of course one of the items that has to be changed as part of a conversion to 12-volt electrics.

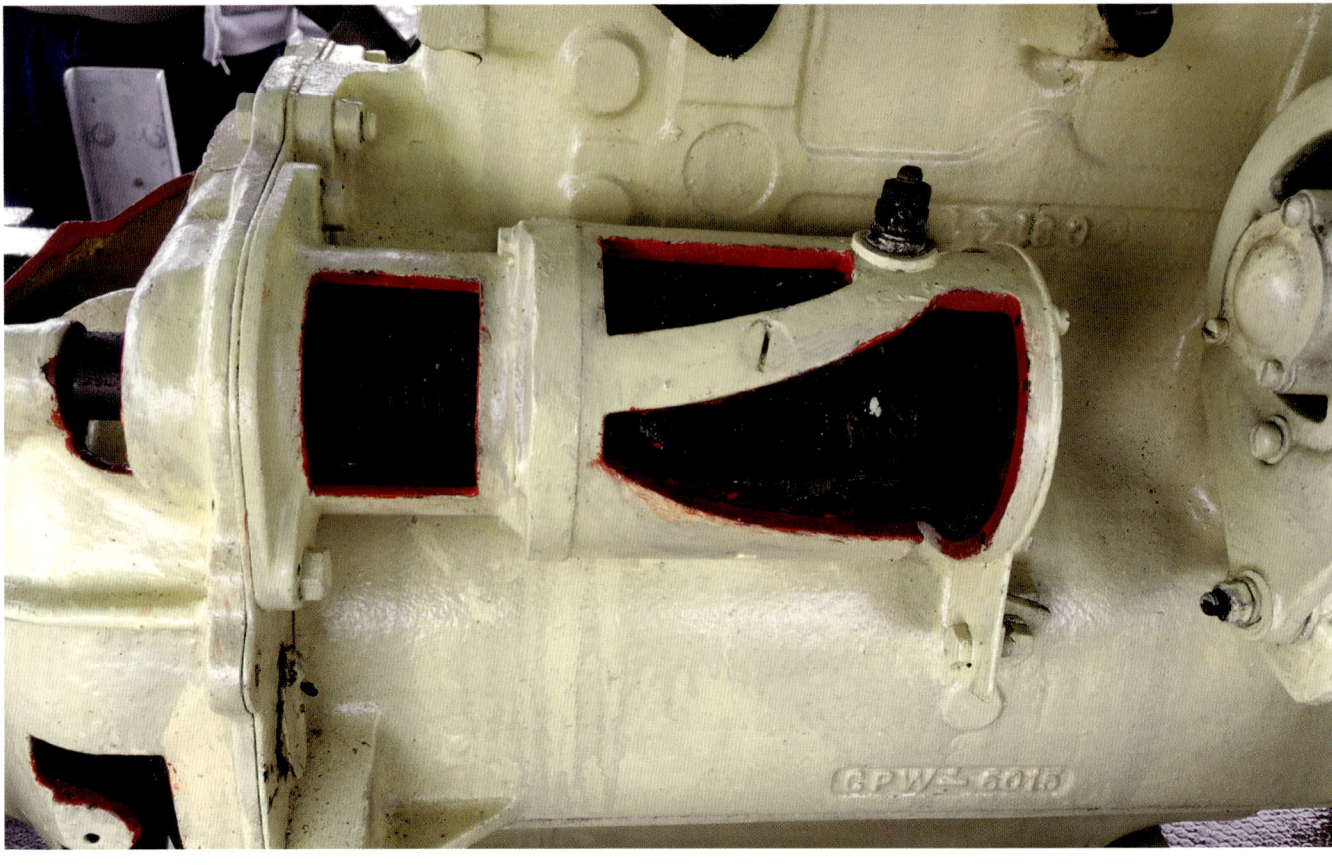

The starter motor is seen here in cutaway form on a REME instructional chassis. As the casting number makes clear, this is a Ford engine. Colours were added for clarity in training, not for authenticity!

STARTING & IGNITION SYSTEMS

Starter motor
The starter motor is another Autolite item, with part number MZ-4113. This has a black-finished body with a large metal identification tag. Modern reproductions are available, and it is also possible to find reproductions of the original motor that are modified to suit 12-volt electrical systems.

Distributor
The standard distributors were made by Autolite, and have top-entry caps in brown plastic. The distributor body was always finished in Satin Black when these items were new.

Two types of distributor were fitted. The early one had Autolite part number IGC-4705, and the later one was taller and dustproofed, with part number IAD4008. Willys changed to the later type from March or April 1944, and Ford followed suit in mid-June the same year.

Ignition leads
The spark plug leads and ignition king lead were always black with a glossy finish that tends to degrade quite quickly. The spark plug leads on early engines have a conical protector cover at the plug end, which is sometimes described as a drain shield. These were made of brown Bakelite on 1942 and some 1943 engines. Willys switched to black rubber shields during 1943 but Ford appears to have stopped fitting the shields altogether at about the same time. There remain some controversies and unanswered questions about precise originality in this area.

Coil
The coil is mounted in a bracket on the right-hand side of the cylinder block towards the rear. All coils originally had a black metal body and a black Bakelite top, but inevitably there was more than one type over the years. Research continues into the minutiae of these items, but what follows appears to be broadly correct.

Willys MBs used a coil made by Autolite, with part number IG4070L. The casing (usually) had the Autolite name pressed into it. Up to serial number MB 288835 in December 1943, the coil had an earthing terminal on the bottom; thereafter it did not.

Early Ford GPW coils have no manufacturer's markings but, like the MB coil, they have an earth stud on the bottom. The casing carries a date of manufacture and is stamped with the F script. Coils from 1944 and 1945 were made by Essex (whose name appears on the casing abbreviated to SX). The 1944 coils have an earthing terminal but the 1945 ones do not. They are again marked with the F script.

LIGHTING

Headlights

The headlights on all Jeeps are mounted behind the grille, and the metal bowl of each one is attached to an arm that is hinged from the top of the grille. This arm allows the headlamp to be swung up to rest on the top of the grille so that its light shines back into the engine bay to aid maintenance work at night. The hinged brackets are handed.

The headlight bowls on Ford Jeeps have an F-script marking, as do the swivel bolts. There are also differences between the two makes in the electrical connector, which is semi-circular on Willys MBs and round on Ford GPWs.

The headlights themselves were originally made by the Corcoran Brown Lamp Company in Cincinnati, Ohio and were 6-volt sealed-beam types with a 5-inch lens diameter. The original glasses carried Seelite brand markings towards the bottom, but there were some variations in the lens design.

The Jeeps delivered to the Canadian Army from February 1942 (beginning with number MB 118600) were fitted with crude headlamp guards, consisting of two metal strips bent and welded together.

Marker lights

All Jeeps have blackout marker lights mounted within the grille and below the headlamps. They have a diffused, low intensity beam. There were two main types of these. The Willys type has a round mounting plinth and is stamped CB (for Corcoran Brown) on the metal front face. By contrast, the Ford type has a teardrop-shaped plinth and has the ubiquitous script F stamped into its front face. In January 1942, after building 8430 MB Jeeps, Willys added a toothed lock washer to the marker light mounting pads to improve earthing (grounding).

Front blackout driving light

The earliest Jeeps had no blackout driving light on the driver's side front wing (fender), but one was made available as a field modification. The blackout light then became standard in July 1942 at MB 163750; it became standard on Ford-built Jeeps either the same month or in August.

The light unit itself is a 6-volt sealed-beam type with a metal diffuser assembly that causes it to throw a horizontal low-intensity light. Three different types were used, branded CB (Corcoran Brown), Harley-Davidson, or (inevitably) with the script F for Ford. These blackout lights also had a retaining

The main elements of the front lighting system are visible in this picture of a 1945 Ford GPW. Below the five-inch round sealed-beam headlamp is the small blackout marker lamp, and on the wing is the larger blackout driving lamp.

FACTORY-ORIGINAL WARTIME JEEPS

The headlight units were mounted on pivoted brackets so that they could be swung up to shed light into the engine bay for maintenance work in the dark.

Wiring for the blackout driving lamp was fed neatly through the wing to meet the main harness that ran across the inner wing panel.

The blackout driving lamp became standard in late 1942 but was available on request before that. The guard ring was part of the mounting bracket assembly that was bolted to the wing.

ring which came in two types, one with a single screw fixing and the other with three fixing screws.

All lights have a guard ring that is bolted to the wing top, and there are two different types. The early one is known as the "tombstone" type and is quite rare, as it was part of the field modification kit. It has straight sides and a different mounting base from the later type, with differently spaced bolt holes. As this was not fitted on production, there appear to be none with the F-script marking associated with a Ford-manufactured part. The later type of guard ring is known as the "horseshoe" type, and tapers inwards towards the bottom like a horseshoe. Those fitted in the Ford factories do have an F-script marking.

Reflectors

Not strictly part of the lighting system, the reflectors fitted to Jeeps nevertheless served an important function in identifying the position of a vehicle.

All Jeeps carried four red reflectors, two mounted next to the tail lights on the rear panel and one mounted on each side of the body behind the rear wheelarch. All were attached by two screws. The side reflectors were always mounted with the screws at 12 o'clock and six o'clock, but the rear reflectors commonly had them at 1 o'clock and 7 o'clock, to keep them clear of a panel join.

The subject of reflectors has been a minefield for some time, and experts continue to debate what was fitted and when. Broadly speaking, it seems that Willys always used reflectors with a round metal rim and that Ford used round ones on early vehicles but later moved to oval rims (typically marked with an F-script stamp) and to a "trimmed" or clipped oval rim. It may be that different Ford assembly plants used different types after the change from round rims. Presumably there was less metal in these later rims, and that would have appealed to Ford if it made them cheaper!

The rims were made by various companies. The round type that Willys used was made by Corcoran Brown and is marked "Corcoran Brown Plastic no 100". Early Fords had one marked "Guide A-2 no 408C" and "Made in USA", typically with an F-script marking as well. The later clipped-rim reflectors have "Guide A-2 no 415A" (sometimes only "Guide A-2" without the number) and "Made in USA" on their rims.

The reflector inserts were all made of plastic. The early Willys Corcoran Brown rims typically came with inserts marked "Tiger-Ey" that were made by the Do-Ray Lamp Company. Later ones had inserts marked "Stimsonite no 12". The early Ford reflectors were also the Tiger-Ey type, but from around March 1942 changed to the Stimsonite type.

In all these things, it is important to remember that motor pools charged with field repairs would have fitted whatever came to hand and would not have attempted to preserve factory "originality".

Just visible around the rear light unit of this 1942 Ford GPW is the rubber sealing ring that was later discontinued. Both reflectors should be red; the one on the body side appears orange in this photograph.

The round type of reflector rim is seen here on a 1942 Willys MB.

Ford used reflectors with two differently shaped rims on later models. This 1945 example shows the oval or elliptical type.

FACTORY-ORIGINAL WARTIME JEEPS

The other type of reflector rim used on late Fords was this "clipped" type, again seen on a 1945 model. The rubber seal around the tail-light would not have been an original fitting on a Jeep built as late as this one.

At the rear left corner of the same Jeep are the trailer electrical socket with its spring cover and the standard military-pattern rear light unit. The reflector has an elliptical frame and a Grotelite reflector, neither of which would have been fitted at the factory, although the bolt fixings are factory-correct.

Tail lights

The tail lamps are separate light units that are bolted to the MB Jeep's rear panel. Willys used Corcoran Brown units which have embossed CB lettering on the face panel, while Ford made their own which carry a script F marking.

Both left-hand and right-hand lamps have a red glass lens in the upper section and a letter-box shaped blackout lens lower down. The right-hand lamp contains a blackout stop lamp in its upper section, but the left-hand lamp has only a standard tail marker lamp.

Early tail lights were fitted with a large rubber grommet running around the body. Following the summer 1942 decree that less rubber should be used, Willys stopped fitting these in September, and Ford did the same a little later when their factories ran out of stocks of the rubber grommet.

Trailer socket

A Warner trailer socket was added to the left-hand side of the tail panel during July 1942 on Willys production, and slightly later on Ford production. Before this, a socket had been available for fitting in the field. The first Willys to have it as standard was MB 158372.

These sockets have the Warner name stamped into the outer rim. They were plated from new and the rim was initially left unpainted while the sprung cover was painted in Olive Drab (or otherwise to match the main body colour). However, it seems that the unpainted rim was normally painted over in service. The ones fitted by Ford seem not to have been given a F-script identification.

HORN

There has been considerable controversy about the Jeep horn, which is mounted on the engine side of the cowl, ahead of the driver. The parts manuals show that two main types were used, both made of metal and painted black, and both with a long trumpet. Mounting brackets differed between Willys and Ford models, the Willys type having a plain fold and the Ford type having a distinct V in the fold; in addition, the Ford ones always carried a script "F" logo.

One type of horn is known as the Sparton, which was the brand name of its manufacturer, Sparks Withington of Jackson, Michigan. It had the company's part number B-9427. The other type of horn was made by the Schwarze Electrical Company and was a model 61, with part number 61400. These horns appear to have been fitted interchangeably, although some authorities believe that the Schwarze horn was originally associated with Ford models. Schwarze was another

Most Jeeps had this style of horn, with a long trumpet. Note that the ram's horn bracket holding the horn to the bulkhead-mounted bracket on this 1942 Willys model remains correctly unpainted.

The four hex-head bolts and washers on the body side show that this Willys is fitted with the radio junction box.

Michigan company, in this case with headquarters in Adrian.

There are minor differences between the Sparton and Schwarze horns. The trumpet of the Sparton horn is stamped with the Sparton name, which is typically hard to read through the paint, but the Schwarze horn carries no maker's name. The Sparton horn has a deeper flange on the horn body where the trumpet fits to it, and the Schwarze horn has a screw in the centre of the body at the back where the Sparton type does not. Good reproductions of the Sparton type are available.

It seems likely that some very late production Ford models had a horn with a much shorter trumpet. This is again believed to have been made by Sparton.

RADIO FITTINGS

From March 1943, Jeeps were fitted as standard with a radio junction box that was located on the inside of the body between the passenger seat and the body side. The box is normally tinned and then painted Olive Drab, and is bolted through the body panel. The first Willys model so fitted was MB 217543.

For more detailed information about Jeep radio fittings, please see Section 7 of this book.

DASH & INTERIOR

Despite the extreme simplicity of the Jeep's interior, there were multiple detail variations over the years of its production. Some, like the addition of a glove box, made a useful difference.

DASH

The dash panel is a simple steel pressing attached to the inner surface of the cowl, and contains the switches, the dial gauges and (on models from February 1942) a lidded storage compartment. The handbrake lever is also mounted through the dash. The turned-over flange at the top of the dash has a cut-out section just above and to the right of the dash light on most models, although this was missing from early models built before November 1941. It was probably introduced to overcome an assembly or manufacturing problem.

Willys and Ford dashes were not exactly the same, and had some differences in their piercings. The GPW dash built after March or April, for example, has a circular hole just to the left of the left-hand dash light. This is normally covered by a steel disc that is tacked behind it. The intention was for the disc to be knocked out when a cold-weather starting kit was fitted.

From June 1944, a first aid kit was mounted to the back of the dash on a bracket. There is more detail about this in Section 7, Additions.

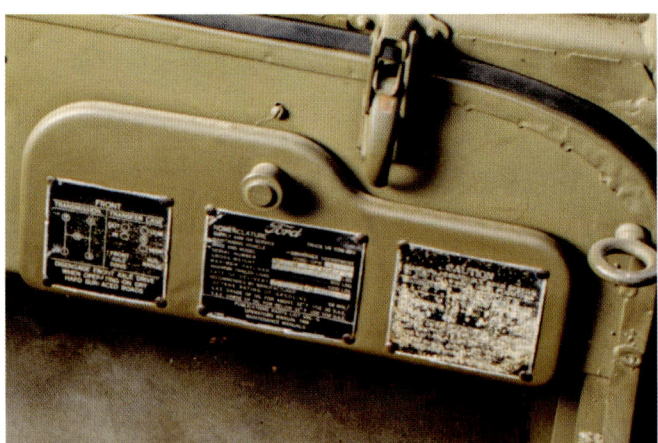

The glove box became standard in February 1942, and was always fitted to Ford GPW models. The button for the latch lock is clearly visible here.

Glove box

The first 20,698 Willys MBs did not have the storage compartment (usually called the "glove box"), which is located at the far right of the dash. It was introduced in February 1942 at serial number 120697 and was intended to carry a gas mask and eye shields. When the glove box was introduced, the fire extinguisher was moved to the driver's side of the vehicle.

The hinged lid of the early glove box has a keylock and a friction spring. This early arrangement was clearly not satisfactory, and a redesigned lid was introduced after only a couple of months, at serial number MB 137909 in April 1942. These later lids have a latch lock mounted higher up than the earlier keylock, a striking plate on the inside, and no friction spring. Interestingly, these later lids still have an indent in the hinge base for the friction spring, even though this had been discontinued, and the indent remained in place until early 1945. This is probably a small illustration of the speed of development: the revised lid must have been designed and its tooling ordered before the decision was taken not to continue using the spring.

Early glove boxes have a rubber seal, but from July 1942 (and Willys serial number 156083), a jute seal was fitted as part of the US military policy to reduce the use of rubber. Early

This cut-out section appeared in the flange at the top of the dash in November 1941. It was presumably introduced to ease manufacture.

DASH & INTERIOR

Three of the gauges are seen here on a later 1942 Willys MB. The speedometer has the early counterbalanced needle, and the fuel gauge is marked as such and has the short needle that reaches only to the base of the scale. The oil pressure gauge correctly reads to 80 psi.

All five gauges are seen here on a 1945 Ford GPW. The speedometer is a Waltham type with the later short needle, and the fuel gauge has the long needle that extends across the scale marked on the instrument's face. The ammeter carries the capital F marking at its base that was characteristic of these instruments – and does not stand for Ford! Both the oil pressure gauge and the engine temperature gauge carry the maker's identification in white lettering around the base of their dials.

These are the very early gauges on a slat-grille Willys MB. The fuel gauge carries the legend "Gas".

Early dials have a stepped bezel that is generally described as a "paint can lid" type, for obvious visual reasons. Later types have a similar but less angular style that is usually described as the "rounded edge" type. The change took place in approximately February-March 1942 but was probably made gradually and was not tied to specific serial numbers; it is also likely that some vehicles may have had examples of both types during the changeover period.

Ford GPW models have a rubber seal, which is glued to the bulkhead. For the same reasons as Willys, they changed the seal, although possibly not until about November 1942. The later Ford glove boxes have a cork seal, which is glued to the inside of the glove box lid.

There are other differences between the Willys and Ford glove boxes. The Willys type has a flat floor but the Ford one has two stiffening swages that run from front the rear. The later "latch lock" lids have a stepped bezel and a plain press-button release, which was never changed on the Ford GPW. From late 1944, however, Willys changed to a plain bezel and added the world PUSH in capitals.

Gauges

There is a cluster of five dial gauges on the Jeep's dashboard. The largest of these is the speedometer, which is in the centre. Around these (clockwise, from top left) are a fuel gauge, an ammeter, a coolant temperature gauge and an oil pressure gauge. As usual, there were multiple variations on production between 1941 and 1945; and, as usual, there is a great deal of conflicting information available about what went on and when. The guidance that follows should therefore not be considered definitive but rather part of a work in progress.

Willys

Dealing first with the Willys MB, all speedometers read to 60mph and have both an elapsed distance recorder and a trip counter. Slat-grille models and a few early pressed-grille models were built with a distinctive Autolite SPK-4001B speedometer that is marked only in 5mph increments. However, when a revised speedometer with markings in 1mph increments was introduced in April 1942, it appears that an order went out to change the early speedometers to the latest type on vehicles already in service. As a result, few of these early speedometers survive. Replacement speedometers included an AC type with stepped bezel that was not used on production models, but many were probably replaced with one of the standard production-type speedometers of the time.

From April 1942 (and Willys serial number 137760), the new speedometer had 1mph marking increments and a white-painted counterbalance on the needle; it is generally called the "long needle" type. There were initially two suppliers of these speedometers, which were Stewart-Warner and King Seely.

The next change came in February 1943. The speedometers from the two existing suppliers changed to a "short needle" type, with a black circle in the centre and no counterbalance. At the same time, Waltham became a third supplier of speedometers, but these Waltham speedometers had a "long" or counterbalanced needle. The Waltham speedometers were probably purchased to overcome a shortage, and had probably all been used up by about August 1943.

From that point on, Willys continued to fit the "short needle" speedometers from Stewart-Warner and King Seely until the end of production. Waltham meanwhile re-entered the picture in about April 1944 with its own speedometer to the "short needle" specification.

The needle of the fuel gauge points upwards and the gauge is marked "Fuel", although early examples fitted to the slat-grille MB are marked "Gas". Early pressed-grille models from February-March 1942 have a Stewart-Warner fuel gauge with a "paint can lid" bezel. Between March 1942 and April 1943, the bezel changed to the round type and the Stewart-Warner gauge had a long needle that extended over the graduated scale at the top of the dial. After that, a "short needle" version of the same instrument was supplied, with a needle that was only just long enough to reach the graduated scale.

The ammeter also has a needle that points upwards, and was always supplied by Stewart-Warner. Both slat-grille and early pressed-grille MBs (to March 1942) had a gauge with a "paint can lid" bezel, its face being marked from -30 to +30 amps. The ammeters fitted between March 1942 and August 1943 had a rounded bezel, their faces were marked from -50 to +50 amps, and there was a long needle that extended over the graduated scale at the top of the dial. From then on, Stewart-Warner supplied a "short needle" version of the same gauge, normally marked "SW 403398 Made in USA" at the bottom of the face.

The oil pressure gauge reads from 0 to 80 pounds per square inch. Most were made by Stewart-Warner, although Autolite gauges of a similar specification were also fitted between March 1942 and January 1943. The early Stewart-Warner gauges used in February-March 1942 had a "paint can lid" bezel, but all gauges after that had rounded bezels. The needles were always counterbalanced until August 1943, when a short-needle type was introduced. All oil pressure gauges operate by means of a capillary tube.

The engine temperature gauge reads from 100 degrees to 220 degrees (in Fahrenheit), and most were made by Stewart-Warner. These gauges register temperature by means of a capillary tube attached to their body. Changes in production were the same as those for the oil pressure gauge: the bezel changed from stepped to plain in March 1942, there was dual-sourcing of Stewart-Warner and Autolite gauges between March 1942 and January 1943, and a short-needle type introduced in August 1943 was then used until the end of production.

Ford

Ford predictably did things their own way. Some early-1942 GPW models had a King Seely KS-40363BM speedometer marked to 65mph, but Ford soon changed to a 60mph type in line with the Willys specification. Like Willys, Ford fitted both Stewart-Warner and King Seely speedometers, but the early 1942 types were distinctive in having black numerals on a white background for the odometer and trip counter, instead of the white on black type used by Willys. The early Stewart-Warner speedometer with this specification was a model 400096.

By the summer of 1942, and most likely earlier, Ford speedometers were either a Stewart-Warner 403261 or a King Seely KS-40363-C. Both had "long" needles and white on black numerals in the distance readouts. "Short-needle" speedometers probably arrived at the same time as on Willys models, around February 1943, and at the same time Ford began to use a Waltham speedometer, which remained in use alongside the others until the end of production. The final type of King Seely speedometer had model number KS-40363N.

Ford fuel gauges were made by Stewart-Warner and had the long needle up to February 1943 and the short needle thereafter. Very early examples had a "paint can lid" bezel, but as on Willys production this soon gave way to a plain bezel.

Ammeters were again of Stewart-Warner manufacture, and all were marked from -50 to +50. Most GPWs had the long-needle type, with no maker's name visible on the face, but later models had the "short needle" type marked "SW 403398 Made in USA". This later type may have been introduced for the GPW at the same time as for the Willys MB, in autumn 1943, but some experts believe it did not reach Ford production lines until 1945. As for the fuel gauge, very early models had an ammeter with a "paint can lid" bezel but the plain type was introduced probably in March 1942.

The oil pressure gauge was probably always a Stewart-Warner type, with a "paint can lid" bezel in February-March

DASH & INTERIOR

The left-hand dash lamp here has the extension piece. The one on the right does not, but does show the slit in the shield through which light came. The fuel gauge here has the short needle, but the ammeter has the long type.

Both dash lamps here are fitted with extension pieces.

1942 and a rounded bezel thereafter. Needles were probably always counterbalanced, and these gauges were probably always marked "SW 402693 Made in USA" at the bottom of the face. They had the same 0 to 80 pounds per square inch scale as their counterparts in Willys MB models.

Finally, the engine temperature gauge was again made by Stewart-Warner and was marked from 100 degrees to 220 degrees. The bezel changed from the early to the round type in March 1942. Probably all these gauges were marked "Stewart-Warner 400083 Made in USA" at the bottom of the face, and probably all had a counterbalanced needle.

Dash lamp

There are two dash lamps, which are mounted just above the fuel gauge and the ammeter. They have push-fit metal "shields", with a small slit that allows the light to shine directly downwards on to the instrument dials. The shields could be fitted with extension sections that move the light further out from the dashboard – but are not much liked because they make the shields very easy to knock off in everyday use.

Switches

The switches are mounted on the driver's side of the dashboard. There are typically four of them, with round grips. From the left, they are for the lights, the choke, the throttle and the panel lights. All initially had metal grips, with raised letters marked in white to indicate the function of the switch. Inevitably, the white paint tended to wear off over time, and it was probably this that persuaded Willys to change in January 1943 to plastic grips with the lettering moulded into them and then filled with white paint. Ford nevertheless continued with the older style of metal grips, probably reasoning that most Jeeps would not last long enough in service to worry about the paint wearing

off! Some of these switches were also used on other US military vehicles of the time.

Early models also had a simple ignition switch in front of the driver, next to the choke control. (The starter button was always separate.) This ignition switch took a standard H-700 key. Willys and Ford types were essentially the same, although the Willys keylock had a smooth bezel while Ford fitted a serrated bezel that made it easier to grip during installation or removal.

However, it soon became clear that drivers were following civilian practice and removing the keys, leaving the vehicles unusable. As a result, a keyless system was introduced, with

These are the dash switches on a slat-grille Willys MB, which also has a keylock for the ignition. The function of each control is clearly labelled.

A later collection of switches and controls is seen here on a 1945 Ford GPW. The lighting switch is quite different, with a much more comprehensive set of positions, and there is a simple toggle switch in place of the ignition keylock.

BO DR
The letters stand for Blackout Drive and this position gives the blackout lights front and rear, including the blackout brake light.

BO MK
The letters stand for Blackout Markers and this position gives the front and rear blackout marker lights only, without the wing-mounted blackout headlamp.

OFF
The topmost position switches all vehicle lights out of circuit.

STP LT
The letters stand for Stop Light, and this position switches all vehicle lights out of circuit except for the brake lights.

HD LTS
The letters stand for Highway Driving Lights, and this position allows the use of all the vehicle's lights for normal road work.

There were changes to the bracket assembly for the choke lever and to the throttle shaft and lever in approximately December 1941. The change took place somewhere around Willys serial number 104000; John Farley has narrowed it down and suggests that the changeover point was serial number 103468.

Data plates

From the start of production, all MB Jeeps had three data plates attached to the glove box lid. The plate on the left carried a schematic diagram of the transmission lever positions; the one in the centre was the Nomenclature plate; and the one on the right was a warning plate giving maximum road speeds in each gear and advice on draining the cooling system.

a simple toggle switch in place of the keylock. This became standard in January 1943 at Willys serial number 202023. Ford changed over to a similar toggle switch at the same time, once again preferring a serrated bezel to the smooth Willys type. Worth noting is that some owners of otherwise carefully restored Jeeps today prefer to use a key-operated ignition switch to reduce the risk of theft or tampering at shows.

The early light switch is a simple push-pull on/off type, and on those models with a blackout driving lamp it is accompanied by an extra switch mounted just above it that is labelled "B.O. Drive". Willys used a switch made by the Douglas Manufacturing Co of Bronson, Michigan, while Ford switches came from Cole Hersee in Boston.

From June 1944 on Willys Jeeps and probably from July on the Ford GPW, a more complex single lighting switch replaced the two separate earlier ones. This is generally described as the rotary type and has a short lever that moves against a plate marked with five different positions. The plates on Willys switches are made of aluminium and printed green, while those on Fords are made of black plastic. The five switch positions are as follows.

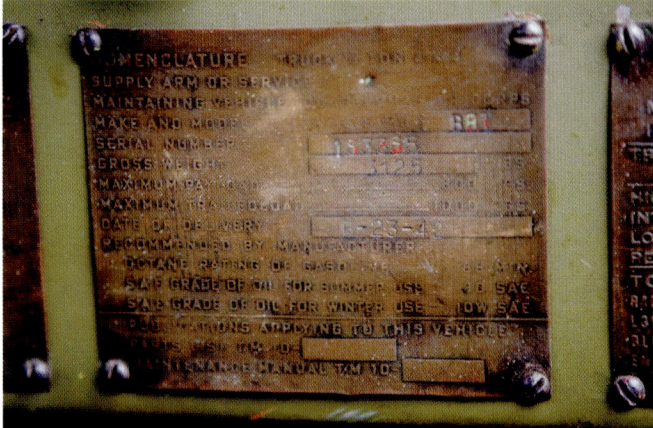

This is an early Willys plate, showing the vehicle serial number as 153355. The multi-coloured paint is probably a relic of post-war civilian usage before the vehicle became a treasured historical artefact! This plate is worn and the description "Willys MB" is only just visible in the fourth row of the inscription. The date of delivery is shown as 6-23-42 (23 June 1942).

DASH & INTERIOR

Early Ford data plates are seen here in situ. They were made of brass and were originally attached by screws; the pop-rivets used to hold these to the glove-box lid are not original.

All three plates were attached by four fixings to the metalwork behind; as explained below, the fixings themselves changed over the years. The three plates were joined in May 1944 (Willys) or July 1944 (Ford) by a fourth or "shipping" plate, which gave dimensions and weights. This was attached to the dashboard on the left of the glove box, again by four fixings. Ford shipping plates had a clear border around the black printed section, but the Willys plates did not.

The transmission, warning, and shipping plates did not change visually, although the material from which they were made did change in line with changes made to the Nomenclature plate. There were multiple different versions of the Nomenclature plate, as outlined below.

Willys Nomenclature plates

The earliest Willys plates were made of brass, showed the model as a Willys MB, and showed the supplying arm as the Quartermaster Corps. Early plates have two blank panels at the top right, but from March 1942 a third blank panel was added next to the Willys MB name.

There were special versions of these on Jeeps destined for Canada, Russia and China. The Canadian plates used from February 1942 had a completely different design, and there was a further new design for Canada from April 1942. Early Russian deliveries had standard data plates, but a Russian-language version was produced from March 1942; the first 250 Jeeps for China that month had standard data plates but the remaining 670 had a special Chinese-language plate. The Russian-language plate appears to have been altered during April 1942 and Russian deliveries over the next couple of months had this revised version.

This is a good reproduction of the later 1942 Willys plate, correctly attached with screws. It shows the serial number as 186313 and the date of delivery as 11-1-42 (1 November 1942). This style of plate was used from around July 1942.

Willys introduced a third type of standard Nomenclature plate in July 1942. This was made from zinc-coated steel rather than brass, and carried the Willys logo prominently at the top. This visual change was probably a response to the military instruction to remove the Willys name from the tail panel of the body: Willys wanted to make sure their name remained

This close-up of the Nomenclature plate reveals that the vehicle is a Ford GPW with serial number 38688 and that it was delivered on 6-10-42 (10 June 1942).

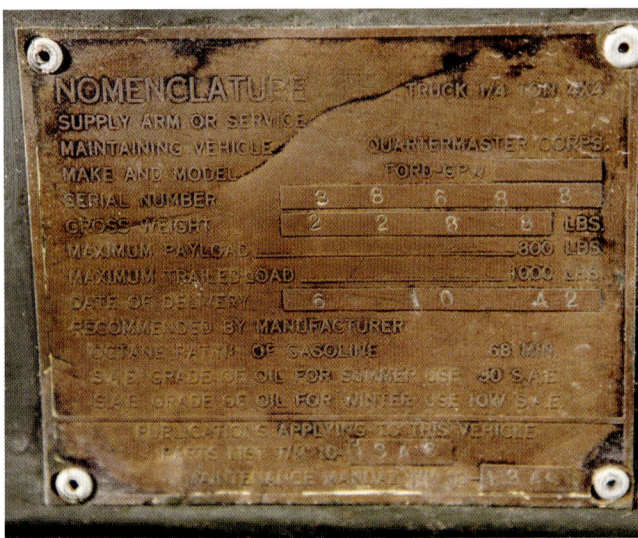

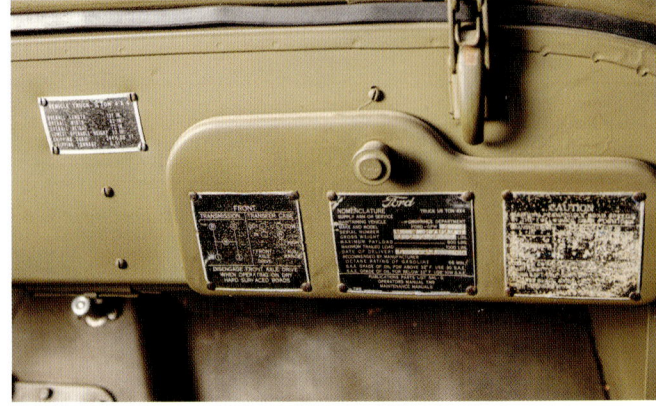

The three data plates were joined during 1944 by a fourth plate with shipping details. This picture of a 1945 Ford GPW shows its correct location.

Again attached with non-original fixings, these plates on a 1942 GPW retain some of the black printing, which makes them considerably easier to read. In this case, the serial number is 66807 and the date of delivery is 9-22-42 (22 September 1942).

Properly attached with screws this time, these are reproduction plates on a 1942 Ford GPW. The details of serial number and date of delivery have not yet been stamped into them.

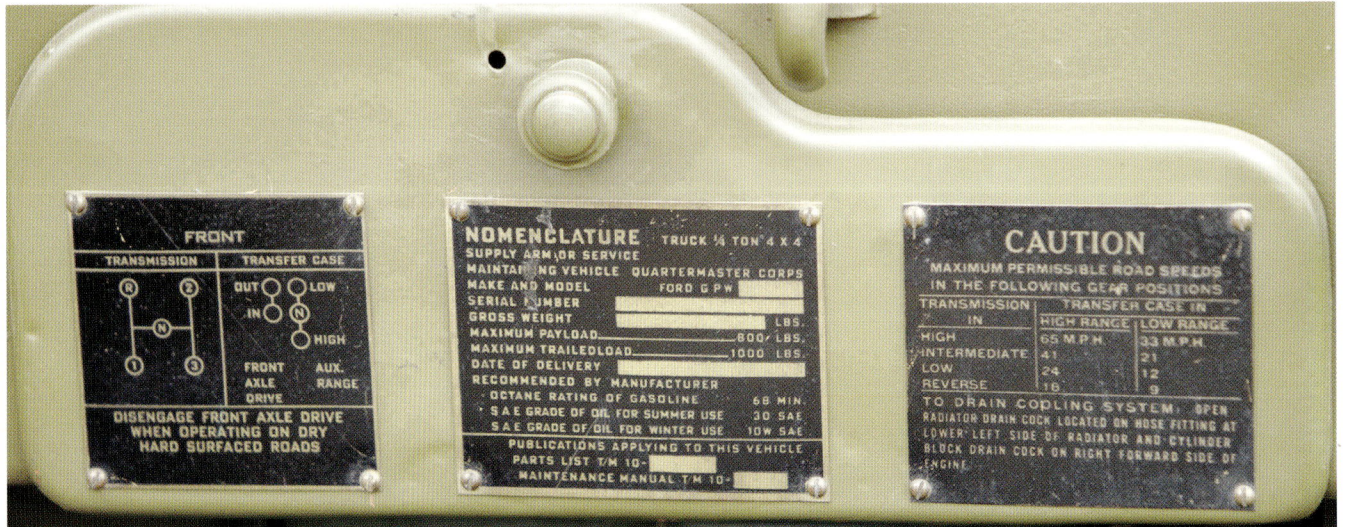

DASH & INTERIOR

This close-up shows the shipping plate on a 1945 GPW.

This appears to be a genuine original Nomenclature plate for a 1945 Ford GPW. It shows the serial number as 270334 and gives the date of delivery as 5-31-45 (31 May 1945).

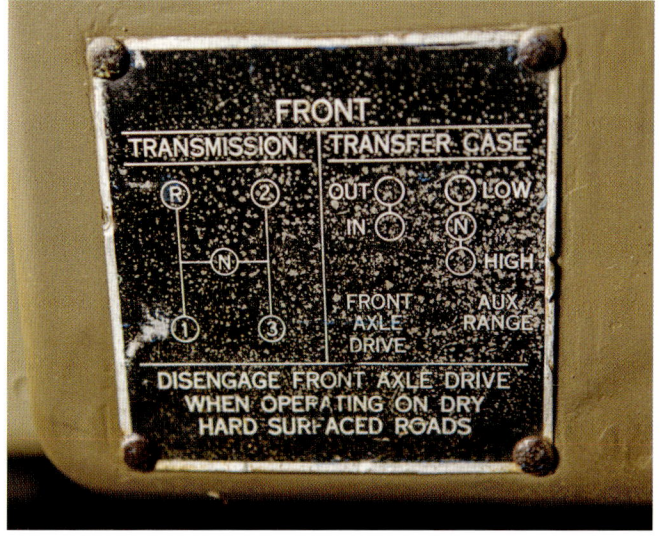

From mid-1942, plates were made of zinc-coated steel. It may be that the rivets fixing this one on the 1945 GPW are original.

somewhere on the vehicles they built. The new Nomenclature plate was nevertheless flanked by the brass versions of the other two plates until stocks of these were exhausted. They then changed to zinc-coated steel to match the Nomenclature plate.

A fourth type of plate followed during December 1942. This was again made of zinc and was visually similar to the third type, except that Ordnance Department replaced Quartermaster Corps as the supplying arm – a bureaucratic change that actually occurred in mid-December. From early October 1943, these plates began to appear with an Ordnance Department "crossed cannons" logo or cartouche stamped into their faces just below the Ordnance Department words. However, it is by no means certain that this appeared on every vehicle.

The final change to the Willys plates occurred in early March 1945. This new type was again made from zinc. The Willys logo disappeared from the top of the plate and the manufacturers' name was now shown a few lines lower down as Willys Overland Motors Inc, Jeep Division. The Ordnance Department stamp was also relocated lower down, cutting across the blank panel for Maximum Weight.

Ford Nomenclature plates

Ford Nomenclature plates were of course different again, and among other things showed the vehicle type as a Ford GPW. When makers' names were banned from the tail panels in spring 1942, Ford took a little longer than Willys to react but had a new plate with its name at the top in production during September that year. The Ford plates in use during 1942 were made of brass, as were their Willys contemporaries.

Ford's third type of Nomenclature plate arrived in January 1943, and was distinguished by being made of steel and showing the Ordnance Department as the supplying arm instead of the Quartermaster Corps. The other data plates on Ford Jeeps switched to steel at the same time. This type of plate continued in use until the end of 1943, but for 1944 Ford changed the material again and all further plates until the end of production were made from aluminium. It is not clear whether an Ordnance Department cartouche was added to the plate on some vehicles from autumn 1943, as was the case with the Willys plates.

Data plate fixings

The three main data plates on Willys models were initially screwed to the dash panel (or glove box lid) by plated plan-head self-tapping screws. On later vehicles, a change was made to machine screws with special stamped nuts behind the panel.

Ford always used rivets to attach their data plates. The brass plates were attached by brass-plated steel rivets, but the later zinc-coated steel and aluminium plates were attached by cadmium-plated rivets.

The shipping plates were probably always attached by screws on both Willys and Ford models.

The early type of steering wheel with its large hub and wide spokes is seen here on a 1942 Ford GPW.

This close-up of the large hub and generously-proportioned spokes shows the early steering wheel on a slat-grille Willys MB. Note that this wheel is black.

MAJOR CONTROLS

Steering column and steering wheel

The steering column is clamped to the bulkhead, with a rubber bush inside the clamp on the earliest models but a webbing bush from September 1942 on both Willys and Ford models.

All steering wheels have three spokes and a small horn in the centre boss. They should be fitted with one spoke in the six o-clock position and the other two at 10 o'clock and 2 o'clock. However, there were several different types of steering wheel.

The earliest style of wheel fitted to the slat-grille Willys models has a large centre ring and was made from black thermoset plastic by Sheller, whose name is moulded into the underside of one of the spokes. These wheels were also used on early pressed-grille models from both Willys and Ford.

A second type of wheel was introduced in March 1942 on both Willys and Ford models, with the same design but now manufactured by Sheller from green Tenite (a thermoplastic material). These wheels have 5/16in plugs in holes on the back of the spokes. Some experts add that from MB 17307 in August 1942 the size of these holes and plugs was reduced to 1/8in, but there appears not to have been a similar change on the wheels that Ford fitted.

The third type of steering wheel was introduced in September 1942 for both Ford and Willys models. The changeover point on Willys models was MB 202023. This third type was a physically different design with metal spokes, a much smaller centre ring and a composite rim. (The composite is widely rumoured to be soya bean extract!). All these wheels were painted Olive Drab. Small numbers have supposedly been found with an F marking (a block letter, not the Ford script) on the underside of the hub, but the significance of this is not clear.

Some authorities believe that Willys briefly used a fourth type of wheel in early 1942, just before the arrival of the green Sheller wheel. This was the same as the green Sheller wheel, with 5/16in holes and plugs, but was made of black Tenite.

The late style of steering wheel was distinctively different, with a small hub and narrow metal spokes.

DASH & INTERIOR

The handbrake lever is mounted through the dash, and its grip was intended to hang downwards like this. In the picture, the handbrake is "on", and the grip is pulled out from the dash.

The early type of rubber gaiters and their retaining rings are seen here on a 1942 Ford GPW.

Handbrake

The handbrake is mounted through the dash and has a simple pistol-type grip that was designed to hang downwards. There is a groove within the handle, and Ford-manufactured grips have an F script logo within the groove. The handbrake acts directly on the parking brake at the back of the transmission by means of a cable, and there is a retracting spring to ensure correct functioning of the whole mechanism. This retracting spring was changed for one with increased tension in December 1941 at Willys serial number 102731.

Gear levers

The main gear lever is on the floor in the centre of the vehicle; on the MA Jeeps it was mounted on the steering column. There are two additional shorter levers, the one nearer to the driver for selection of drive to the front axle, and the one further away giving a choice of Low or High range gears in the transfer box. All three levers have ball-type grips in black plastic with threaded brass inserts that allow them to be screwed to the gear levers. The three grips are all the same size.

On Willys models, the front axle drive selector lever is straight and the High-Low selector is bent. From serial number 10100 in November 1941, larger-diameter levers became standard, and at the same time a grease nipple was added to the transfer case lever pivot pin. On early models of both Willys and Ford, all three levers have rubber boots (gaiters) that are secured in place by rings bolted over the boot and to the floor; the boot for the main lever is much larger than those for the other two. These boots were normally left in their natural black rubber state, but from mid-1942 some Willys boots may have been painted Olive Drab. On both Willys and Ford models, the rubber boots were replaced by suede leather gaiters during October 1942.

These are the later suede leather gaiters on a 1945 GPW. The retaining rings have an interesting and non-original selection of fixings!

FACTORY-ORIGINAL WARTIME JEEPS

The early Willys pedals had a rectangular clutch pedal while the brake pedal had a rounded end. Both had a "pebbled" finish and a raised edge to prevent the driver's foot from slipping off the pedal. These are seen on a slat-grille MB.

The clutch pedal gained a rounded end in early 1942, and all Ford GPW models had this configuration. The large round button is the foot-rest, and the floor-mounted starter button is just visible on the right of this picture.

Pedals and starter switch

The starter is operated by a press-switch mounted on the floor to the driver's side of the vehicle centre-line. It was designed to be operated by foot after the ignition had first been turned on by the dashboard switch (or keylock, on early models). At least two types of switch were used. Early ones have a simple "tower" but later ones have a "hat" and look similar to the dip-switch. These later ones were made by Douglas Manufacturing and were probably introduced during 1945.

The accelerator pedal is a simple metal pressing that pivots on floor brackets at its lower edge. On early Jeeps, it had a rubber seal around the linkage, but this changed in September 1942 (at serial number MB 176601) to a leather one. The only other change during production came in April 1943 when the connection between pedal and accelerator linkage was revised. Early pedals had a rubber fitting on the back, into which the linkage's ball pivot fitted. With effect from serial number MB 225209, a metal fitting was used on the back of the pedal instead. Both of these changes were of course brought about by the restriction on the use of rubber after mid-1942. Willys painted the pedal and all its linkages in Olive Drab, but Ford used a cadmium-plated linkage arm to the carburettor and a black Parkerised return spring.

The clutch and brake pedals on Willys models were always made of steel, but Ford made theirs from cast iron. Clutch pedals have a raised right-hand edge to prevent the driver's foot from slipping off, and brake pedals have a raised left-hand edge for the same reason. Up to summer 1944, all pedals also had "pebbled" surfaces to provide extra grip.

Very early Willys models have a rectangular clutch pedal, while the brake pedal has a rounded right-hand end. From late February or March 1942, the clutch pedal was given a rounded left-hand end that matched the one on the brake pedal. Ford

DASH & INTERIOR

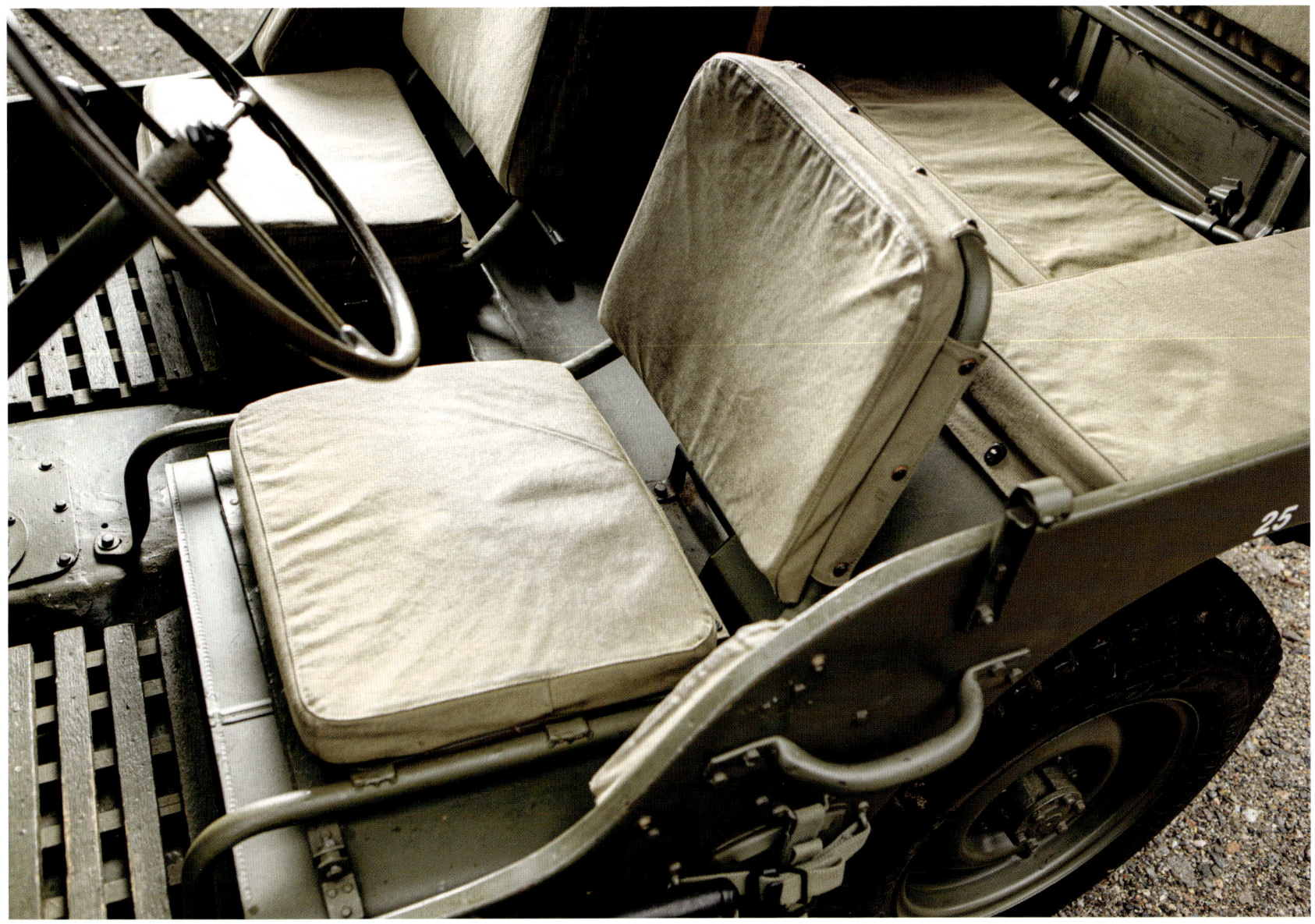

clutch and brake pedals both had rounded ends from the beginning, and were distinguished by an F script marking on their shafts.

Then from June 1944, the Willys pedals changed from steel castings to steel pressings, losing their "pebbled" surfaces in favour of a surface covering in a coarse-surfaced paint called Grip-Tite. The Ford pedals nevertheless retained their existing configuration with the "pebbled" finish until the end of production.

On all models, there is a button-like foot rest bolted to the transmission cover just to the right of the accelerator pedal.

Fire extinguisher

The fire extinguisher is covered in the seventh section of this book, Additions.

SEATS

All Jeeps have two tubular-framed front seats and a rear bench seat. The floor section between the seats was used as stowage in a variety of different ways, to suit the needs of the users. The British Army, for example, often bolted an ammunition box to the floor in that position.

From June 1944, three pairs of spaced-out holes were drilled into the floor under the passenger seat, and were fitted on production with six nuts and bolts. These were provided in anticipation of the decontaminator unit and its bracket which was soon to become available to order through the US Ordnance Department. (Section 7, Additions, has more information about the decontaminator units.)

Seat covers were in Olive Drab canvas, and the screws and washers that attached them originally had a black oxide finish.

Both front seats have tubular steel frames. The driver's side frame is much larger than the one for the passenger's side because it has to straddle the fuel tank.

The shorter passenger's side seat frame is clear in this picture.

The pressed backrests of the front seats have side-to-side reinforcing "ribs" and remain uncovered.

Front seats

The two front seats have tubular frames, but these are quite different from one another. The driver's seat frame extends forwards in front of the cushion in order to clear the petrol tank. The passenger's seat has a shorter frame that bolts to the floor near the front of the cushion, and is mounted on pivots so that it can be tilted forwards to improve access to the rear.

The driver's seat also has a special pan with an opening to give access to the fuel filler underneath. Early seat pans have a smaller opening than the late type, where a larger opening was used to suit the larger filler neck used from September 1942. Meanwhile, the frame of the passenger seat is fitted with four footman loops made from brass and coated black. These loops are accompanied by webbing straps which are designed to secure the canvas roof under the seat when it is not erected. Each strap has a U-shaped metal tip at one end and a black-coated brass buckle at the other.

Early Willys front seats are distinguished by a join in the tubular section at the top; these are generally known as "split-frame" seats. Ford seats did not have this join, and the Willys seats changed to the Ford type when the composite body was

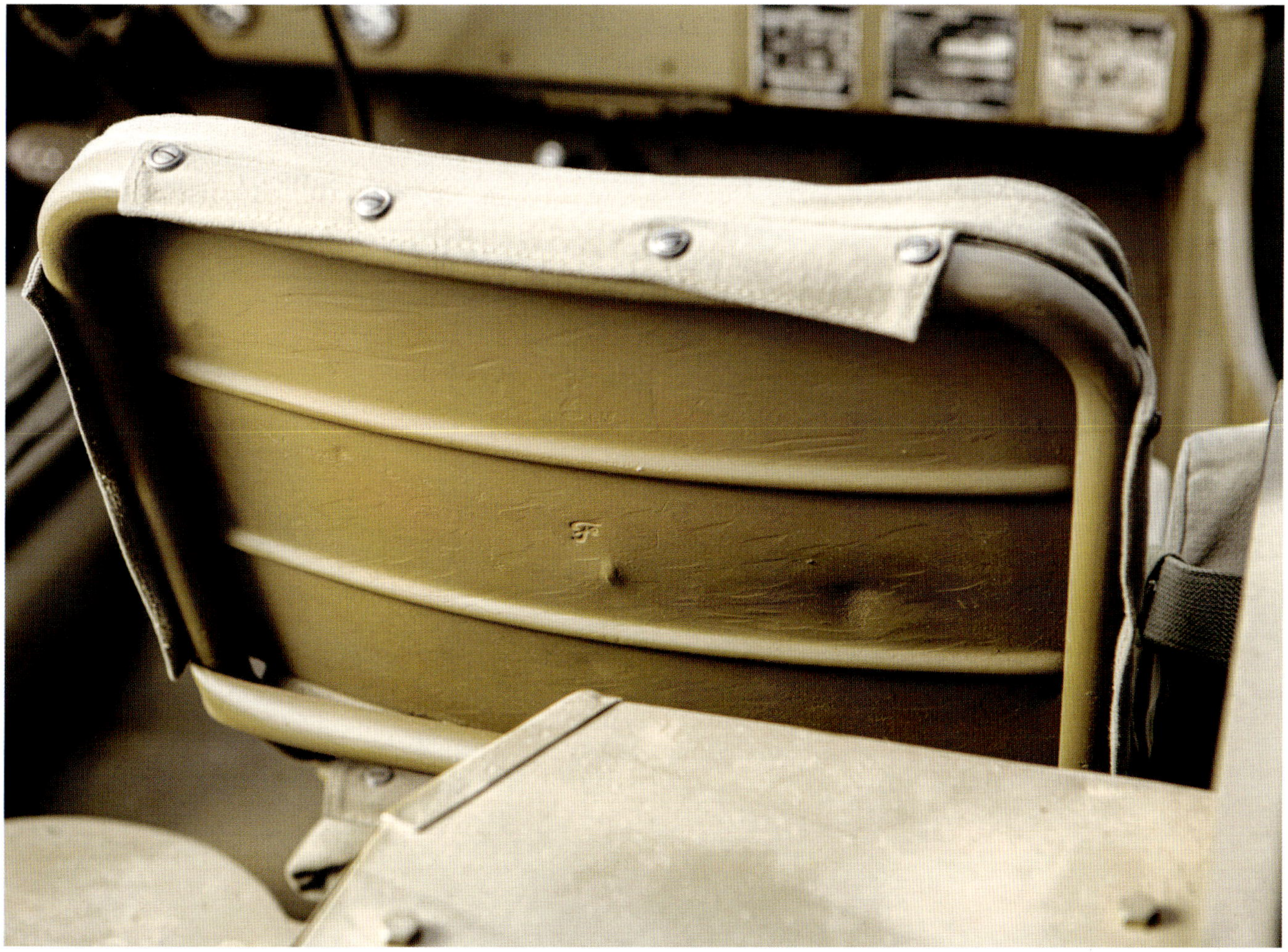

DASH & INTERIOR

It should come as no surprise that Ford stamped their identity into the backrests of the seats that they manufactured.

The early Willys seats have a "split frame", with a very visible join at the top of the backrest frame. This one is on a slat-grille model.

Cushions are held in place by screws passing through eyelets in the cloth.

The rear seat in position: the backrest could be folded down or the cushion could be folded up, to give more space for carrying equipment in the rear. The bracket visible beside the right-hand body brace in this picture is for the starting handle.

introduced in early 1944.

Seat cushions were upholstered in heavyweight, water-repellent, fire resistant cotton duck. Very early cushions contained a 2-inch thick foam rubber pad, but from approximately December 1941 this was changed to a horsehair pad covered in rubber. When it became policy to conserve rubber, there was a further change to springs and felt from September 1942. On these cushions, the springs are readily visible through the upholstered covering.

Early seat cushions have a zip in the bottom to create a stowage pocket. The user handbook could be stored there, and in service soldiers sometimes improved comfort by stuffing a blanket into the pocket. However, by July 1943 it was clear that the zipped pocket was an unnecessary luxury, and so it was deleted.

Rear seat

The rear seat is a bench type, with a foldable backrest and separate cushions for the seat itself and the backrest. The backrest can be folded down by disengaging it from a pair of hook-type brackets, and the cushion can be folded forwards so that the steel seat pan below can be used as a carrying platform. The hook-type backrest retaining brackets differ between Willys and Ford models, the Willys type having a more angular shape and the Ford type being more rounded and also slightly thicker. Ford backrests and seat pans are marked with the F script logo, and the backrest hooks are marked with a block F.

In December 1942 at serial number MB 193040, two brackets were added to the underside of the rear seat cushion. One was for the handle of the tyre pump and the other for its base. Further brackets were added later, with an ear-shaped tab

The rear seat cushion could be folded up out of the way. The brackets visible on the underside of the seat pan here are for the tyre pump, which is illustrated in Section 2 on the Body.

Maximum versatility: the rear seat cushion could also be folded forwards to leave the pressed steel pan for carrying loads.

that has a hole in the centre, allowing the pump hose to be secured by its valve jet.

The British military modified the uprights of the rear seat backrest, and there is more about this and associated British modifications in the Appendix.

Early models – this is a 1942 GPW – have a zipped pocket under the front seat cushion. In this case, it forms a home for the maintenance manual.

ENGINE & TRANSMISSION

The Jeep name is cast into the late Willys cylinder heads. Like all Willys heads, this one would originally have been painted Olive Drab.

Those late Willys heads also had the Willys name cast into them, but Willys never branded everything as effectively as Ford did.

ENGINE

Although Ford and Willys engines were built to a common design so that parts from one were fully interchangeable with parts from the other, the two engines were not exactly the same. During 1943, a comparison was made between examples of each, and this revealed that the Willys engine was 10 lb heavier than the Ford – no doubt because Ford had been able to shave weight off here and there as they had adapted the design for production in their factories.

Rather more embarrassingly for Ford, the comparison also showed that the dipstick on their engine was set too low by 3/8in, which led to false dipstick readings suggesting there was more oil in the engine than was actually the case. Ford also changed the design of some of their engine castings late in 1944, and as a result the Ford engines manufactured during the last six weeks of that year and in 1945 are said (probably mainly by Willys devotees) to have been sub-standard.

The engine was of course a Willys design, and it had started life as long ago as 1926 as the four-cylinder engine of the Willys Whippet car. Its design was conventional for the time, with an iron block and head, three main bearings, a chain-driven camshaft and an L-head design with pushrod-operated side valves. It was a long-stroke (undersquare) design, with a swept volume of 134.2 cubic inches – 2199cc in metric measurements – and was known to Willys as the L134 or Go-Devil engine. More importantly, it had proved to be a robust engine and was therefore still in production in 1938, which is when the basic revisions that created the Jeep engine were made.

What Willys wanted in 1938 was an updated and more powerful version of the engine that would put out more than the 48bhp of the version then in production. So Barney Roos, who had become Willys' Vice President and Chief Engineer that year, improved it with larger inlet ports and a new inlet manifold; he added a stronger crankshaft and replaced the cast iron pistons with aluminium ones that carried three rings, delivered a higher compression ratio and now rode on forged steel conrods; he also reduced the weight of the flywheel and aimed for closer production tolerances. The result was an engine that delivered 60bhp

Willys engines were always finished in Olive Drab, as seen in this 1942 model. The two bolt holes on the inner wing further from the camera are for the regulator box, which has been removed on this example during conversion to a 12-volt electrical system.

for the 1939-season Willys Model 39.

This updated engine, then, was the basis of the one that became the Jeep powerplant. In its 1940 specification for the Quarter-Ton military vehicle, the Quartermaster Corps had called for just 85 lb ft of torque at the axle, which was no problem for the Willys engine because it boasted 105 lb ft at the flywheel. So the changes that Roos had to make for the Jeep engine were quite limited: he switched to a Carter carburettor that would allow the engine to keep running on a 20-degree side slope or a 56-degree front-to-rear slope, and he added an engine governor to limit the maximum crankshaft speed to 3800rpm. With 60bhp at 3600rpm and 105 lb ft at 2000rpm, the engine easily met and actually exceeded the specifications that the QMC had called for.

All wartime Jeeps had a version of this engine, whether built by Willys or by Ford. The engine was always mounted slightly left of centre in the chassis – which caused braking difficulties until the suspension was revised in mid-1942 (see Section 6). All engines have a cast-iron head with the combustion chambers cast into it. The head gasket was originally a thick sandwich type of copper and asbestos. The cylinder block is also cast iron, with the cylinder bores machined directly into the block and a detachable side cover plate that gives access to the valve gear. Of interest is that bare cylinder blocks have now been remanufactured in the USA. Their tolerances are claimed to be better than those of the originals, and they are also made of stronger material.

The crankshaft is forged from nickel-chrome steel, heat treated and machined. It runs in three white metal bearings with steel backings and a lining of "white" Babbitt alloy. A thrust washer and shims, mounted between the front main bearing and the timing sprocket, take care of crankshaft end thrust. The main journals are cross-drilled, and the diagonal drilling feeds lubricant through the crankshaft webs to the big ends. The flywheel is a steel casting that was balanced during manufacture, and its steel ring gear was shrunk in place.

The connecting rods are I-section steel forgings with lengthwise drillings to provide lubrication and a bleed hole to feed oil to the cylinder walls. Pistons are made from aluminium alloy and are tin-plated. They have two compression rings (the lower one with a tapered face) and one oil control ring. Oversizes from 0.10in to 0.40in were available to suit rebored cylinder blocks.

Both inlet and exhaust valves are located in the cylinder block and run in cast-iron guides. They have single return springs with conical cotters and are operated by mushroom-head tappets actuated directly by the camshaft. Self-locking adjusting screws for the tappets allow valve clearances to be set accurately. The camshaft is made from nickel steel and runs in four bearings, three of which are formed within the crankcase while the fourth, at the front, is press-fitted and staked into place.

The camshaft was always chain-driven, by way of a sprocket at its front end. The timing chain has no tensioner. Camshaft end float is controlled by a plunger and spring at the front end. The camshaft has an eccentric to drive the fuel pump, and incorporates a skew (spiral) gear that drives the oil pump. The distributor is driven from a dog gear on the oil pump.

The oil pump itself is driven by planetary gears and its cover has a cylindrical plunger-type spring relief valve (which can be adjusted by means of shims). The oil filter is a standard external US military-pattern "junior" by-pass type, with a replaceable element.

Willys engines
The L-head design of the engine means that both inlet and exhaust valves are in the cylinder block. The crankshaft has three main bearings, and the camshaft is driven by a roller chain.

Serial number
The serial or identification number of a Willys engine is stamped into a machined pad on a rounded boss on the passenger (right) side of the cylinder block, near the front and just below the cylinder head, behind the oil filter. Engine numbers have the format "MB xxxxxx". The six digits of the number do not match the vehicle's chassis number.

Cylinder block
Both cylinder block and cylinder head on Willys engines were originally painted Olive Drab.

All Willys cylinder blocks have the number 638632 cast on the base of the block, which is the casting number. There is also

The Willys casting number and casting date are seen here on a 1942 engine.

a casting date on the base of the block, showing the day of the month and the month but not the year. The format used is not the standard American one with the month first, but instead has the day first. So, for example, 3-9 indicates 3rd September.

The assembly date of the engine is stamped at the base of the block close to the bottom flange to which the sump is bolted, and near to the rear main bearing clamp. This is shown in the American format of month, day and year.

The rear engine plate is drilled to take an engine stay cable, which was installed to prevent the engine from moving forwards under rapid deceleration and allowing the fan blades to hit the radiator. The cable itself runs between this plate and a bracket on the chassis cross-member behind the engine.

Cylinder head
No manufacturer's name was cast into the early cylinder heads. From approximately January 1944, the casting was changed and the names Willys and Jeep were both cast into its top surface in raised letters; the Jeep name is roughly central, between the holes for numbers 2 and 3 spark plugs, and the Willys name is just above the holes for numbers 3 and 4 spark plugs.

Early cylinder heads were bolted to the block all round, but from serial number MB 288835 in December 1943, some of these fixings were replaced by nuts and studs.

Crankshaft and connecting rods
Willys crankshafts were roughly cast (not machined) and never had any counter-weights. This saved time and cost in production. Willys used separate nuts and bolts for the bearing caps.

Bellhousing
This was always painted Olive Drab to match the engine.

Sump (oil pan)
Slat-grille Willys models had a sump with a small plate riveted to its left-hand side around the area of the drain plug; this gave

This view of the right-hand (passenger) side of a Willys engine shows the general layout of the engine bay. Left, on the cowl is the AC fuel filter, and next to the battery is the regulator box – clearly an early type without the ribbed casing. The battery is a six-volt type, and the triangular corners of the correct clamp can be seen. This is a later style of air cleaner canister, with embossed instruction plate, and the oil filter canister is a Purolator type. The lid of the oil filler behind is the second type, with a hooked grip on a deep cap. Just visible is the Autolite label on the starter motor. The clips on the air cleaner hose are correct but the Jubilee clips on the coolant hoses are modern replacements for the originals. The cone-shaped spark plug covers are correct for a Willys engine.

extra thickness into which the plug could be screwed more securely. The sump was later redesigned with thicker metal in this area and no additional plate, and these revised sumps were introduced on production in January 1944 at MB 297089. All sumps were painted to match the rest of the engine, and on Willys were therefore Olive Drab.

Inlet and exhaust manifolds

The inlet and exhaust manifolds are separate castings but meet in the middle to provide a hot-spot for the carburettor. They were painted Olive Drab to match the engine when new.

Carburettor

The carburettor is a Carter W-O 539 S type and is mounted on the cast inlet manifold on the left side of the engine. Its fuel inlet hose is made of braided metal.

Early in production, during December 1941, the position of some carburettor fittings was changed to permit easier access. The fittings affected were the choke lever bracket, the throttle shaft and lever assembly, and the tube clamp assembly. There is no agreement on exactly when this happened. One parts list suggests it happened at vehicle number MB 103468 and another shows it at MB 104000.

Note that the post-war civilian CJ-2A models used a Carter

The Carter carburettor was common to both Willys and Ford engines. This picture of a Willys engine shows how the inlet and exhaust manifolds are mounted. The conical spark plug covers that Willys used are also clear here.

type YF carburettor, which is very similar to but not the same as the wartime W-O 539S. Many Jeeps today have also been fitted with more modern but non-original Solex carburettors, as used on the Hotchkiss M201 (see Appendix).

Air horn and cross-over tube

The air inlet (air horn) is clamped to the top of the carburettor and has a rubber seal there. Its other end is clamped to a tube that runs across the top of the engine to an oil-bath air cleaner on the opposite side of the engine bay. The cross-over tube has a groove in its top surface, and this groove is longer on Willys-made tubes than on those from Ford. Early cross-over tubes were probably finished in black, but it looks as if an Olive Drab finish soon took over.

The cross-over tube is welded to a triangular support bracket, of which there are "tall" and "short" versions. The tall version was designed for use with the original AC air cleaner (see below) and the short one for use with the later Oak type; although the "incorrect" ones can be made to fit, there are some alignment problems!

There is a rubber bellows-type hose between the end of the cross-over tube and the outlet on the air filter casing. This has a hose clamp at each end and was probably always fitted in its natural black rubber state – which probably did not prevent some acquiring a coat of Olive Drab in service.

The screw clamp holding the cross-over tube to the air horn changed in December 1941 at serial number MB 104310. There is some dispute about the differences between early and late types (which had different part numbers), but it looks as if the early type consisted of a solid band and the later type had two wire rings, like the clamps used on water hoses. John Farley also says that the early clamp had an internal diameter of 2 13/32in while the later one had an internal diameter of 2½ in.

From early 1943, Willys engines adopted the Ford arrangement with a shorter air tube that was connected to the air cleaner by a bellows-type hose.

Air cleaner

The first Jeeps had an air cleaner made by the AC Spark Plug Co, with their part number 19386. This then gave way in March 1942, at serial number MB 124309, to an air cleaner made by Oak Products, which had their number 613306. This later air cleaner had a removable cover. Early versions of it had instructions embossed into a plate that was fixed to the body, and on later ones the instructions were pressed directly into the body. There was a change to the air cleaner bracket assembly in February 1943, at MB 208437.

Worth noting is that the standard air cleaner element is very restrictive and that more modern replacements that give a higher air flow (and are invisible when installed) allow the engine to breathe more easily.

Oil filler and dipstick

The oil filler tube is mounted on the right (passenger side) of the engine behind the oil filter, and its cap is attached to the dipstick rod. Three different types were used in production.

The earliest engines have a straight filler tube and a deep cap that pushes onto the tube. The grip on top of this cap is a hook type. The second type of filler tube arrived in January 1942 and is generally described as the funnel type because of its wider bell-mouth that eases filling. It was fitted from the start of Ford engine production and from Willys serial number 114550. The cap is wider to suit the wider tube and is again a push-on type; it is shallower than the first type and also has a smaller hook-type grip.

The third type was then introduced in February 1943, at vehicle serial number MB 208437. The filler tube changed yet again, although it still had a bell-mouth, and the cap was changed to one that screwed into place and was identifiable by a pair of upstanding tags. This final type of filler tube has a nipple attached to a rubber hose that leads to the air filter cross-over tube, and is associated with the PCV system.

The tubes and caps were painted Olive Drab on Willys engines but were painted Grey on Ford engines. Ford dipsticks carry an F script marking, but the filler tubes do not.

Oil filter

The oil filter assembly is a standard military-pattern type found on several other US military vehicles of the period. The visible component is a large black metal canister located on the right (passenger) side of the engine towards the front and supported by a triangular bracket that is bolted to the cylinder head. The renewable filter element itself fits inside this canister. There were two major types of canister, and there is still some controversy about which type was in use at which date; functionally,

ENGINE & TRANSMISSION

Some of the original gold decals are still in place on this Fram filter. Note also the maker's label here, often found on the lower body of the filter.

This is the Fram oil filter, with its rather more conical cover. The gold decals are modern reproductions.

they are of course completely interchangeable.

The earlier type of oil filter assembly is a Purolator type 27078. The assembly consists of the canister itself and a removable lid, which has a hexagon in the centre to aid removal with a spanner. When new, this type would have had a rectangular red decal label on the side of the body and a second decal of similar type on the top cover. The Purolator part number was PD-5106, and this was sometimes found as a rubber-stamped or possibly stencilled silver marking on the top cover. At least some filters were originally marked with white or silver lettering reading "Inlet" (above the inlet connection facing the engine), and lower down "Front" and "Outlet".

The later type of oil filter assembly became standard at some point during 1944 and was manufactured by Fram. It is generally similar in appearance to the earlier type but the removable lid is more obviously conical in shape. When new, these filter assemblies had gold decals on both lid and body, and also a small gold-coloured Fram company badge. The decals seem to have changed over the years, but in some cases, they show the lid to have Fram part number 5241, the body to have part number 5310, and the renewable filter element to have part number 5664.

Fuel pump

The mechanically operated fuel pump is mounted on the left (driver's) side of the cylinder block towards the front of the engine and has a domed top cover. The pump assembly was always made by the AC Spark Plug Company with their part number 153776, and the pipe unions were always made of brass.

Fuel filter

All early Jeeps have a fuel filter mounted on the engine side of the firewall on the passenger's side of the vehicle. This filter was made by the AC Spark Plug Co in Flint, Michigan and is their T-2 type. It has two inlet and two outlet unions and a disc-type strainer inside the casing. The filter casing is cadmium plated and originally had a large decal label; modern reproductions are available with this label faithfully reproduced.

From approximately April 1945, this filter was discontinued on both Willys and Ford models. In its place came a sintered filter inside the petrol tank, and the fuel line was changed so that it ran directly from tank to pump.

Valve cover and crankcase ventilator

There is a detachable valve cover plate on the left (driver's) side of the engine. On the earliest engines, this is attached by a screw at the rear and by a bolt passing through the crankcase ventilator at the front. The rear screw was changed to a bolt after engine number 106694 in December 1941.

The early crankcase ventilator (draft tube) is a short tube with an angled open end that simply vents fumes to the atmosphere below the vehicle. This ventilator was discontinued in early 1943 in favour of a Positive Crankcase Ventilation system; see below.

PCV Valve

All Jeep engines switched to a closed-loop Positive Crankcase Ventilation system in early 1943, with a long pipe running between the valve cover and the inlet manifold. The PCV valve was fitted at the inlet manifold end of the pipe.

Willys first installed these valves at or after serial number MB 208437 in February 1943 and painted them in Olive Drab; the engine number 204040 is also recorded as that start point.

Ford engines were painted grey. This underbonnet view of a 1945 GPW is refreshingly original, with the original 6-volt electrical system still in place.

This is the engine from the REME instructional chassis, and shows the Ford casting identification at the bottom of the block. The sump guard is also visible here. Interestingly, the instructional chassis combines a Ford engine with a Willys chassis!

Ford engines

The Ford-built engines in principle used the same design as the Willys engines and followed the major stages of their evolution. However, there were some differences from time to time. These engines were built in the River Rouge plant at Dearborn.

Very noticeable is that Ford stamped their identity into every conceivable engine part that they manufactured themselves. This takes the form of an F script logo, sometimes a full Ford script logo, sometimes the letters GPW, and sometimes two of these together.

Serial number

The serial number of a Ford engine is stamped into a machined pad in the same location as that on the Willys engines. Engine numbers are all prefixed GPW, and this is followed by a serial number of between one and six digits. There is usually a

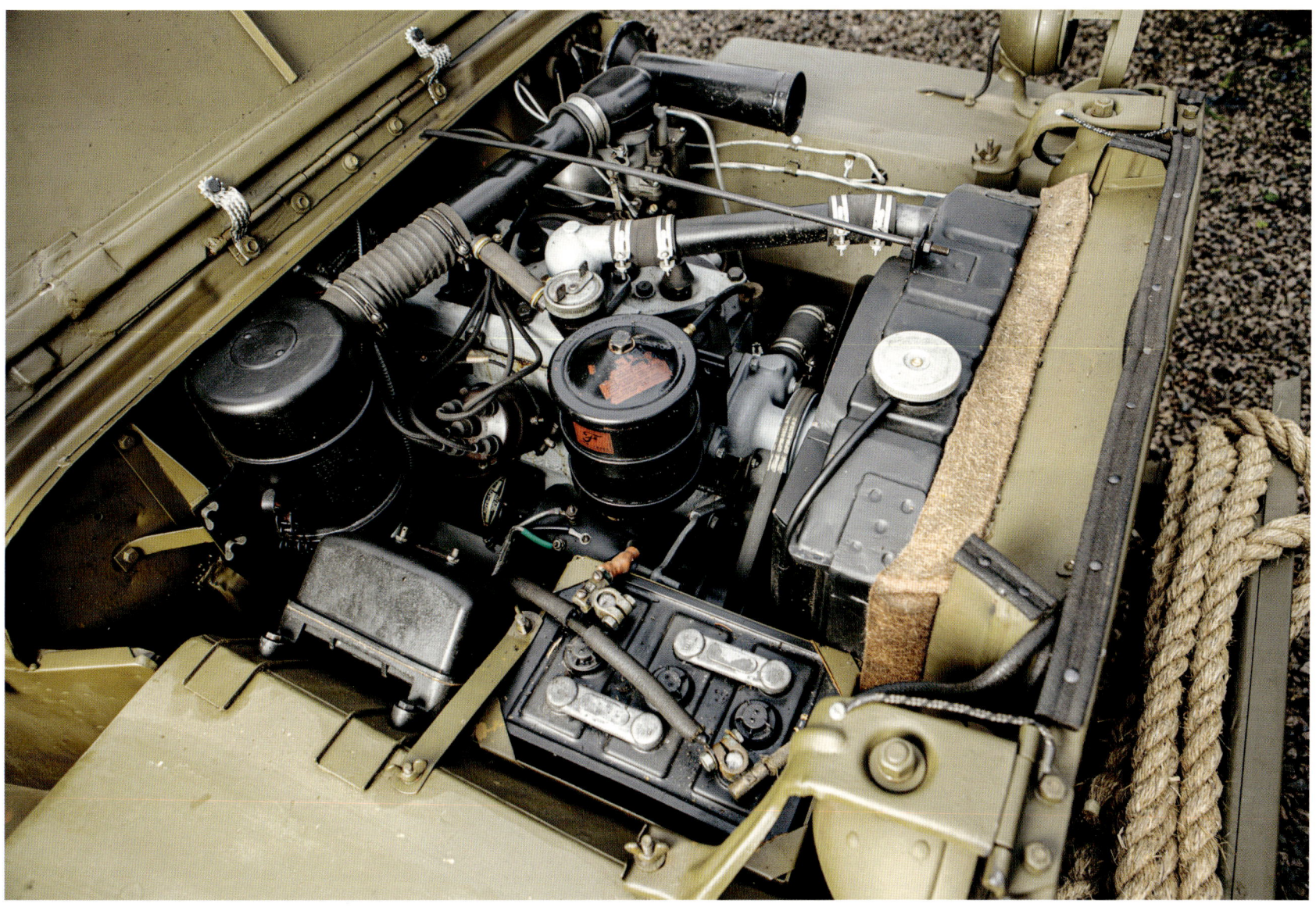

This is the Ford engine in a 1945 Jeep. Although no fuel filter is fitted here, the mounting hole for one can be seen in the front face of the cowl. The regulator box is again an early type with the smooth casing, and has the early type of cork sealing gasket as well. The battery is a six-volt type and retains the correct fixing frame. The air filter canister is the final type, with instructions embossed directly into the casing, and once again an Autolite starter is fitted, as would be normal with a Ford engine. The oil filter is a Purolator type with the remains of an original red decal on the cover; the red decal on the side with with the F script was only found on Ford engines. The oil filler tube behind it is the final type with a lid that has two vertical tags. The hose clips here are period correct, but the spark plug leads have Willys-type covers.

five-pointed star stamped at either end of the number, which was a device to make fraud through alteration of a chassis number more difficult.

The engine number was stamped into the engine when it left the Rouge plant for the Jeep assembly lines. That number was then used as the chassis number of the completed Jeep, with the result that the serial numbers of the engine and chassis originally matched. Non-matching numbers are a clear indication that the engine has been changed – but note that this was not the case with Willys-built models.

Block, head, bellhousing and timing cover

The cylinder block, cylinder head and bellhousing of the Ford engines were always painted grey. The cylinder head is identified by the F script logo under the bracket for the oil filter. The F script logo is also stamped into the timing cover as well as into the bellhousing.

From December 1942, the Ford engines had a redesigned flywheel housing with a boss on the side.

Engine mounting shims

The shims used on the mounts between engine and chassis are stamped with the script F logo in a circle.

These details are on another 1945 Ford GPW. At left is the AC fuel filter, complete with identifying label, and to the right is the later type of regulator box, with ribbed casing. The air filter canister is again the final type, with instructions embossed directly into the casing. The paint on the cylinder head has clearly seen better days!

Engine stay cable
The engine stay cable used with Ford engines was marked with an F script logo.

Crankshaft and connecting rods
Ford claimed that their crankshafts were cast from an alloy steel. They were certainly better finished than the Willys equivalent and incorporated counterweights on the front and rearmost crank webs. The front web was marked with the F script logo. The bearing blocks also carried GPW identification. The Ford bearing caps had integral studs and bolts, in contrast to the separate ones used by Willys.

This was Ford's version of the Purolator oil filter, with the maker's own red labels supplemented by an apparently matching one bearing the F script logo. The cap of the oil filler tube behind has been painted red, which was not standard.

Camshaft and valves
Valves and camshaft followed the Willys pattern, but all were identified with an F script logo. There was one of these on the camshaft drive gear, too.

Sump (oil pan)
The sump is clearly identified as made by Ford and is always painted Grey to match the engine. Early sumps have an F marking on the reinforcing plate around the sump drain hole, and later (from GPW 25755 or GPW 25855 in March 1945) in the metal around it. However, this later type was sometimes obscured by solder during manufacture.

Both the script F and the GPW designation are stamped into the inside surface of the sump, typically on the rear of the baffle plate in the middle and towards the top.

Inlet and exhaust manifolds
The manifolds followed the Willys design but those made by Ford were identified as such and were of course painted Grey to match the rest of the engine. The inlet manifold was identified by the GPW letters (and part number) on the top face of the rear inlet pipe, and by a script F elsewhere. The exhaust manifold had a full Ford logo on its centre section, just above the mounting flange for the downpipe.

Carburettor and air cleaner
Ford engines had the same Carter carburettor as their Willys counterparts. Like the Willys engines, the early Ford ones had an AC pancake type air cleaner; it is an A-183-40 type and is also F-marked. They switched to the Oak type of air cleaner at the same time as Willys, in March 1942. These air cleaners had decal instructions until June or July 1942, followed by a spot-welded instruction plate until October or November that year, and had instructions pressed into the canister thereafter.

Air horn and cross-over tube
The air horn on the carburettor is marked with an F and switched from rubber to felt seals in approximately autumn 1942. Ford engines always had a shorter air tube than Willys types, and this was connected to the air cleaner by a bellows-type hose. This arrangement was presumably found to be superior to the Willys one, and Willys engines adopted it from early 1943.

Oil filler, filter and pump
The oil filler went through the same changes as on the Willys engine, and those changes took place at approximately the same times. Unsurprisingly, the triangular support bracket for the oil filter has an F script stamp on Ford engines, and Ford added their own red decal with the F script to the body of the Purolator filters, which as delivered to them were type PD-5106. Even the oil pump has an F script logo.

ENGINE & TRANSMISSION

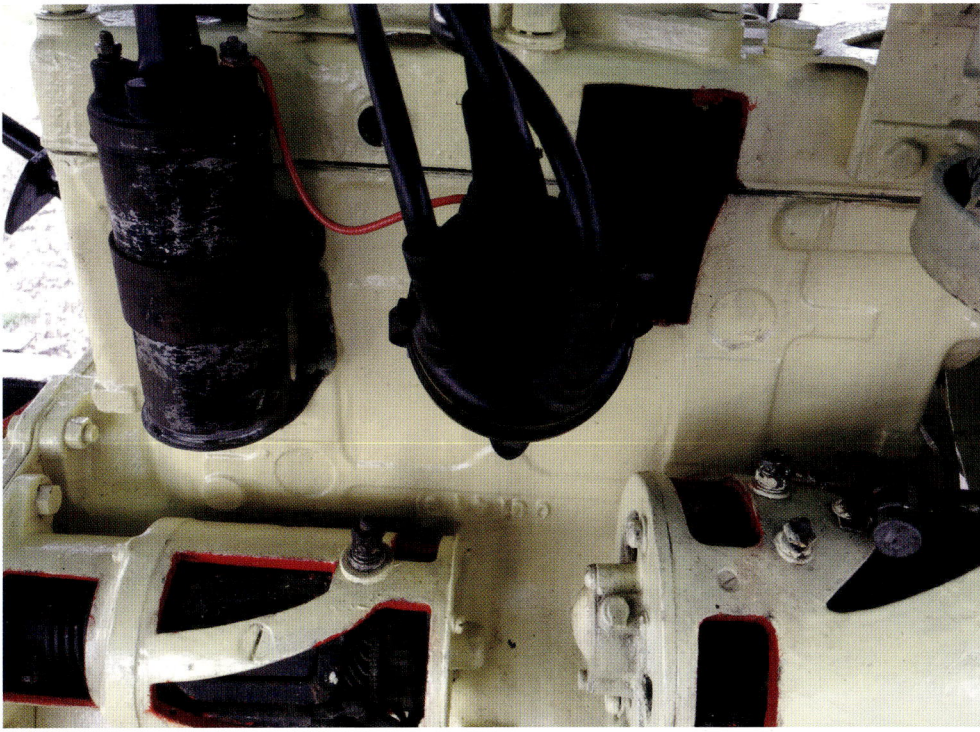

This close-up of the instructional chassis shows the right-hand side of the engine, with the coil mounted in brackets, the distributor, the cutaway starter motor (left) and the cutaway generator (right). The colours were added for clarity during training, and were obviously not those used in production.

On Ford engines, the connections between ignition leads and spark plugs looked like this.

Fuel pump

The fuel pump on Ford engines is the same as the one on Willys engines.

Valve cover, crankcase ventilator and PCV valve

The Ford-manufactured valve cover is stamped with the full Ford script name in the lower section of the pressing. The crankcase ventilation arrangements were the same as on Willys engines and went through the same changes at approximately the same times.

Ford installed a Positive Crankcase Ventilation system in January or February 1943, and in principle this was the same as the one on Willys engines. However, the Ford PCV valves were left unpainted.

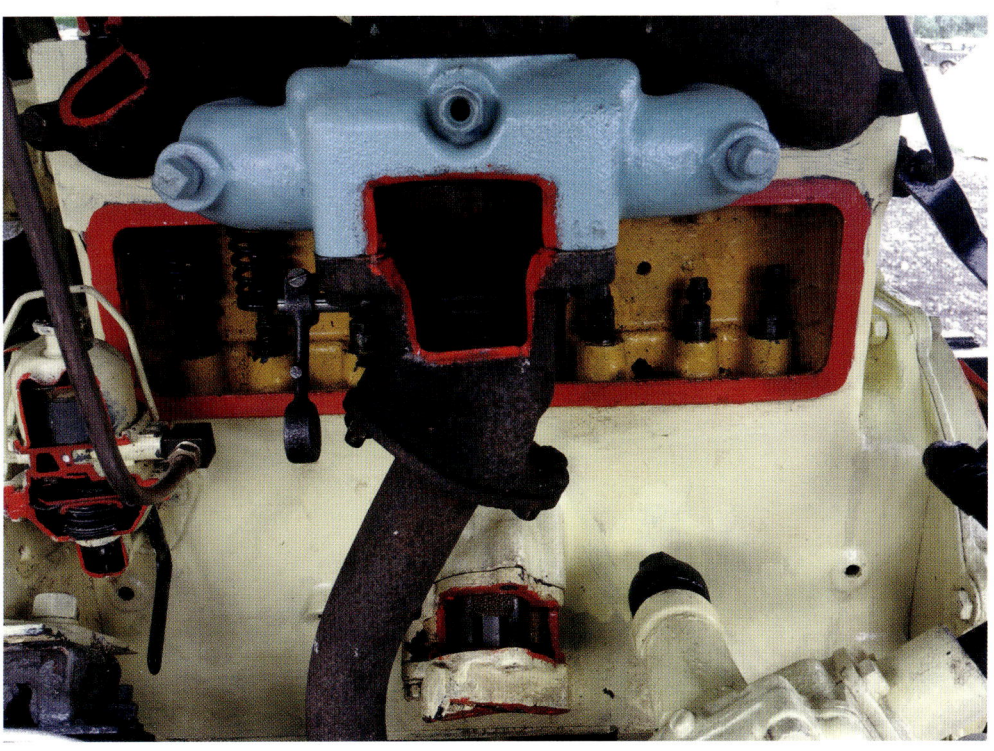

This is the left-hand side of the instructional engine, showing the location of the fuel pump (on the left) and the oil pump (below the exhaust), both of which have been cut away here. The inlet manifold is in light blue and the exhaust manifold has been – rather realistically – left with a rusty surface finish. The engine side plate has been removed to show the valves and, on the left, the valve springs as well. The manifolding has been cut away here to show the hot spot where exhaust heat warms up the air entering the inlet manifold.

COOLING SYSTEM

All these Jeeps have a conventional thermo-syphon cooling system, which has a 22-pint capacity (it was usually described as holding 11 quarts). The water pump is mounted on the front of the cylinder block and has a centrifugal, vane-type impeller. It is driven by the auxiliary belt from the nose of the crankshaft. The thermostat is a conventional bellows type that is designed to keep the engine coolant temperature at 78 degrees Centigrade.

Fan

The fan is mounted on the front of the engine and is driven by a rubber belt. It was made by Hayes and has four blades and a 15-inch diameter. Fans were painted black and those fitted by Ford carried an F identification marking. There is a belt pulley shield attached to the engine sump, which was painted to match the engine: Olive Drab on Willys models and Grey on Fords.

Willys and Ford used essentially the same fan belt but with different part number markings in red. Original Willys belts were marked "Willys A9490", and the Ford belts "GPW 8620-A2". Modern reproductions are available with original style markings.

The spring-loaded generator brace can be pulled up to slacken the fan belt, which prevents the fan from throwing water all over the engine when the vehicle is fording.

Radiator

All radiators have a stay rod that runs above the top of the engine and is bolted to the firewall. This was normally painted Olive Drab. It is not uncommon to find that this stay rod has been bent, typically to give extra clearance above the air inlet cross-tube and prevent fretting. There is also a set of three jute air deflector seals that fit between the grille panel and the top and sides of the radiator.

Willys radiators had a satin black finish and a square-shaped shroud. Early ones had two indentations in the top tank, but later ones had five indentations visible in the front of that tank, with four of them running across the top and down the rear face as well; the change took place at serial number MB 108452 in January 1942. At serial number MB 208452 in February 1943, flanges were added to the radiator to secure the air deflector more effectively. (Note: despite the coincidence of the last five digits, these two serial numbers are correctly shown here.)

The shroud mounted to the back is square overall, to suit the shape of the radiator, with a large circular fan guard. The 4psi radiator cap is a round type with no lugs and original items were manufactured by AC.

Ford radiators appear to have arrived at the Ford assembly plants with a black finish but were painted Olive Drab on production. They were also identified by an F and the letters GPW at the top corner near the tube for the top hose.

The Ford radiator shroud is broadly similar to the Willys type in design but is simpler and contains less metal. Like Willys, Ford initially fitted a round 4psi radiator cap with no lugs, although somewhat inevitably this was given a small F marking. Later Ford caps, of type A-2, did have caps, and also had a larger F-marking.

Some evidence has been found that Willys type radiators were fitted to some Ford GPW models from late 1943 onwards. It may be that different radiators were supplied to different Ford assembly plants in this period.

EXHAUSTS

The most common type of exhaust found on Jeeps is a two-piece system which exits just ahead of the right-hand rear wheelarch. There is a long downpipe from the exhaust manifold, which crosses over to the opposite side of the vehicle and

This is the later type of exhaust tail pipe, with an oval-section silencer (muffler). Earlier models had a cylindrical silencer.

The exhaust pipe crossed under the chassis frame to emerge on the passenger's side; the arrangement can be seen clearly here.

is then attached to a silencer (muffler) with exit pipe. The cross-over arrangement was presumably designed so that the driver was not constantly subjected to exhaust fumes emerging on his side of the vehicle; it would have been much simpler to run the exhaust to an exit on the same side as the exhaust manifold on the engine!

The earliest systems had a cylindrical ("round") silencer but from summer this was changed on both Willys and Ford Jeeps to an oval-section silencer. The changeover on Willys production was made in May at serial number MB 143507 and Ford followed a little later, in July. All silencers were normally painted Olive Drab.

From February 1942, an exhaust guard plate was added, and the under-frame skid plate (see below) was given two extra holes to which the new plate could be bolted. This arrangement lasted until some time in 1943, when a single-piece plate was introduced to do the jobs of skid plate and exhaust guard plate.

A redesigned exhaust system was fitted from some time in 1945, apparently as a result of conditions encountered in northern France after D-Day in June 1944. This was called the deep-mud type but is also known as the rear-exit exhaust. It was probably fitted to Willys models from January 1945 at approximately serial number MB 401550, although some researchers have suggested it was first fitted in December 1944. Ford models appear not to have received it until June 1945, according to Lawrence Nabholtz.

The deep-mud exhaust system consisted of three pieces. First was a flexible downpipe; second came a long intermediate pipe that passed along the left side of the chassis, inside the main rail; and the third section was a silencer (muffler) with tailpipe that was mounted across the rear of the chassis so that the exhaust emerged below the rear cross-member on the right. Official publications do not show very clearly how the system was attached to the chassis and there are differing views on the subject. Many Jeep enthusiasts have in any case preferred to fit the "classic" side exhaust to their late-model Jeeps.

CLUTCH

The clutch was always a cable-operated type with an 8.5-inch diameter. Original clutches were made by Auburn.

GEARBOX (MAIN)

The main gearbox in all MB and GPW Jeeps is Warner model T84J with three forward speeds and one reverse. There is synchromesh only between the second and third speeds, as was common at the time. The actual gear ratios are 2.67:1 (first), 1.56:1 (second), 1.00:1 (third), and 3.55:1 (reverse). Willys always painted the gearbox in Olive Drab, but on Fords it was Grey to match the engine.

There were some minor changes to this gearbox over the years. All early gearboxes had a filler on the right-hand side, but from approximately October 1942 the filler was relocated on the left-hand side. For a time, gearboxes still had a boss on the right of the casing where the original filler had been, but eventually the casting was redesigned and the boss disappeared. Late Ford gearboxes were identified by the GPW letters on their casings. In November 1944, the gearbox oil capacity was increased and the revised gearboxes had a large H cast into the casing to indicate "high capacity". These later casings were also machined to take an additional seal which prevents oil migrating between the gearbox and the transfer box.

The gearbox was always a Warner T84J type. This is an early one, with the variant number T84J-1A cast into its outer casing.

Gearbox and transfer box are seen here installed in the 1942 REME instructional chassis. The gearbox is on the far side, behind the transfer box selector lever.

SKID PLATE

A skid plate is mounted under the transmission to protect it against impacts, and is bolted to a chassis cross-member. There were several different types of plate during production and the type fitted depends on the date of production and on the type of handbrake fitted. All the Willys skid plates have five holes in a row running front to rear, and a pair of holes was added at the side to accommodate the separate exhaust pipe guard introduced in February 1942. Some time in 1943, a one-piece plate was introduced that protected both transmission and exhaust pipe – but confusingly, it retained the same part number (A1253) as the earlier, smaller plate.

A further variant was introduced in September 1944 with a fluted section to accommodate the larger internal expanding brake on the transfer box that was introduced at serial number MB 373337. Very late in production came yet another type of skid plate, this time with a sixth hole, larger than the other five, to accommodate the rubber mounting for the transfer box.

As they so often did, Ford simplified the design from early on, and all GPW models seem to have had a single skid plate with six holes in a row rather than the five on most Willys plates. Two of the six holes are larger than the other four, and a further recognition point is the F script logo stamped into the plate.

TRANSFER BOX (TRANSFER CASE)

All Jeeps have the same two-speed transfer gearbox that has three functions. It transfers the output from the main gearbox to drive both front and rear axles, allows the driver to select either direct (1:1) "road" gearing or low (1.97:1) "off-road" gearing, and selects either all-wheel drive or drive only to the rear wheels. (Low range is only available when four-wheel-drive is engaged, and engagement has to be made with the vehicle stationary.) The transfer gearbox is bolted to the rear of the main gearbox and is arranged so that the propshafts run fore and aft to the axle differentials on the right (passenger) side of the vehicle.

The speedometer drive gear and the transmission handbrake are both mounted on the rear output shaft from the transfer box. On the other side of the transfer box, again at the rear, a bolted cover gives access to a power take-off (which is mainly used to drive an extra generator in some Jeeps equipped with a radio – see Section 7).

This gearbox is one of the most widely-used transfer boxes ever made and enjoyed a very long production run. It is generally known as a Spicer type 18, although strictly it was a product of the Dana Spicer Corporation. Identification tags refer also to Brown-Lipe, which was the gear manufacturing division of Spicer at Toledo in Ohio. These tags are stamped with an identification number which begins with a J and is typically followed by a six-figure serial number. Note that the post-war Spicer 18 gearboxes are broadly similar but have intermediate gear shafts of a larger diameter to give more surface area for the shaft's roller bearings; the intermediate gear shaft in the MB and GPW transfer boxes has a ¾in diameter.

When the Quartermaster Corps compared a Willys and a Ford Jeep during 1943 to check that the planned interchangeability of parts had not been compromised, they discovered that the sliding gear on the Willys transfer case output would not fit the spline of the Ford output shaft. As a result, the shaft of the Willys was "corrected", and was in future made with a slightly smaller diameter.

All transfer boxes, including those on Ford-built Jeeps, were painted in Olive Drab.

PROPELLOR SHAFTS

The propellor shafts are open Spicer Series 1200 types, with needle-roller universal joints at the yokes and a sliding joint.

FUEL TANK

The fuel tank was always located under the driver's seat, and the seat cushion had to be lifted to gain access to the filler. The tank itself is L-shaped and holds 15 US gallons; note that the US gallon is smaller than the Imperial gallon used in the UK, and the capacity to Imperial standards is approximately 12.5 gallons. Tanks were secured by metal straps, with anti-squeak strips to prevent noise from fretting. They were protected on their underside by a separate stone guard that was bolted in place.

Early changes were made in December 1941. At serial number MB 103576, a wood spacer was fitted to the underside of the

The cutaway transfer box on the instructional chassis shows the input gears nearer to the camera, and the output gears further away.

ENGINE & TRANSMISSION

The early fuel tank guard had square edges, as seen on this slat-grille model.

From February 1942, the tank's stone guard had a curved outer edge.

tank shield at the rear of the seat. Slightly later that month, at serial number MB 104433, two stamp nuts were added to the straps securing the tank in place.

The first type of tank fitted came with a small fuel filler cap that clearly proved inadequate, and from serial number MB 174731 in September 1942 a different tank was fitted with a wider opening and an extension pipe to aid filling. There was also a major change to the tank stone guard (visible below the body) from February 1942, when the original square-edged type was replaced by one with rounded edges. The change took place at serial number MB 118600, and coincided with the first Jeep contract for the Canadian Army.

An additional five (US) gallons of petrol could be carried in the jerrycan attached to the rear panel after August 1942. Original US jerrycans came with a flexible filler tube and a screw-on cone filter.

The later type of filler cap was always attached by a chain so that it could not be accidentally left behind!

The early tanks had a small filler orifice and an access hole different in shape from the later standard type. Also visible here is the fuel gauge sender unit.

This type of fuel filler became the production standard, with a larger-diameter neck and correspondingly larger access hole.

CHASSIS, SUSPENSION, WHEELS

CHASSIS FRAME

The basic design of the Jeep's chassis frame remained unchanged throughout wartime production of the MB and GPW. When the US QMC compared a Willys and a Ford Jeep during 1943 to check that minor changes made by each manufacturer had not compromised standardisation, they are said to have discovered that the radiator bracket holes on the front frame of the Ford were 1/8in too small but that they could easily be adapted in the field. This was an impressive demonstration of the similarity between the two makers' products.

The chassis is a conventional ladder-frame, with channel-section side members, three bracing crossmembers and an additional crossmember at the rear which extends beyond the side members to support the rear of the body. Welded to the centre of the third crossmember is a roughly circular plate with four holes drilled in it, which was designed to support a

The Jeep chassis was very basic, and even flimsy to look at, but it proved extremely rugged. This 1945 chassis gives an overall picture of the layout.

CHASSIS, SUSPENSION, WHEELS

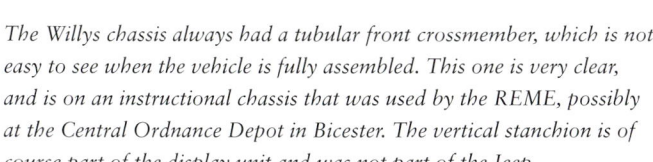

The Willys chassis always had a tubular front crossmember, which is not easy to see when the vehicle is fully assembled. This one is very clear, and is on an instructional chassis that was used by the REME, possibly at the Central Ordnance Depot in Bicester. The vertical stanchion is of course part of the display unit and was not part of the Jeep.

pedestal mount for a machine-gun. There is also a V-shaped reinforcement behind the third crossmember to support the rear body tub and give additional strength for mounting a tow hitch. The front bumper is bolted to gussets mounted to the dumb-irons, effectively creating an additional crossmember at the front of the chassis frame.

Willys had their chassis frames manufactured for them by Midland Steel at Cleveland, Ohio. Ford had the necessary resources to undertake manufacture of its own chassis frames, but insisted on producing its own version of the Willys design, making a number of production engineering changes which, in typical Ford fashion, would save time or costs, or both.

However, the Ford chassis design had not been signed off by the time Ford was ready to begin Jeep production, and as a result the first Ford Jeeps (at least 2200 of them, built up to March 1942) actually had Willys-pattern frames from Midland Steel that were stamped with the Ford chassis number. Ford then began to use its own chassis, but Willys continued to use frames to their original design, still built by Midland Steel, until Jeep MB production ended in 1945. It is not possible to identify a precise changeover point at which the Ford GPW began to use a Ford-built chassis; GPW models were assembled at several different plants, each of which changed over to the new chassis at a different serial number.

There were several differences between the Willys and Ford versions of the chassis. The best-known of these is the front crossmember. Willys used a tubular type, but Ford designed their own U-shaped component, which was fitted with the open side facing downwards. Willys chassis have an additional cross-brace where the legs of the V-shaped reinforcement meet the chassis side rails (so making the V into a triangle). On a Willys chassis, the legs of the V are plain channel sections, but on the Ford chassis there are four holes in each leg.

Three other differences between the two types of chassis lie in the front bumper gussets (bolted to the front ends of the frame's side members), the shock absorber mountings, and the machine-gun mounting plate.

The side-members of the chassis frame were of open channel-section steel, with a reinforcing section riveted inside. The multiple holes in the inner section reduced weight without materially reducing strength.

Ford simplified the design of the front crossmember, using a pressed steel U-section type. Here it is on a 1942 GPW model.

Inevitably, Ford "signed" the pressed crossmember with their script "F" logo.

The Ford bumper gussets have one less hole than their Willys equivalents, and also carry the F script stamp. The Willys shock absorber mountings are made from a section of steel 'U' channel, slightly wider than the chassis, allowing two legs of the 'U' to pass down the sides of the chassis to be welded. The round section bar that the shock absorber fits on to passes through the top of the channel. The Ford GPW shock absorber mountings are two-piece pressed steel types riveted to the chassis, and have the Ford script 'F' stamped into the outer flange. As for the machine-gun mounting plate, the Willys version is more obviously rounded than the Ford type, which is also stamped with a script F. In addition, most of the fixing bolts on Ford chassis have an F script logo on their heads, and that F script logo is stamped into several other places as well.

Common to all chassis frames is a battery support platform that is mounted on the passenger (right-hand) side at the front. Very early battery support platforms came in two pieces, but a one-piece type became standard in February 1942 at MB 120700. At the same time, the earth strap moved from its original position under the battery to a hole drilled in the support assembly.

There were no significant changes to the chassis design during production of the MB and GPW, although in July 1944 a gusset was added at the rear of the frame to prevent cracking.

This close-up of the front end of the chassis shows various mounting brackets, including those for the dampers and the engine.

Clear in this picture are the curved shackle arms to which the front ends of the springs are attached.

Here is the Ford script logo again, this time on one of the bumper gussets at the front of the chassis....

... and here it is again on the other bumper gusset. Note that the logo was stamped in at a different angle here!

CHASSIS, SUSPENSION, WHEELS

The radiator mounting brackets can be seen from this angle, and the layout of the steering is clear, with the steering box at bottom right.

FRONT BUMPER

The front bumper is a simple channel-section pressing that is bolted to the front dumb-irons. It has a hole for the starting-handle and is reinforced in the centre by a block of redwood, also drilled to allow the starting handle to pass through.

Willys and Ford front bumpers differ. The Ford version has a hole in line with each chassis leg but the Willys does not; and of course, the Ford bumper also has an F script logo on its rear face.

The rear of the chassis was deliberately designed to give a strong mounting point for a tow hitch, above and separate from the rear crossmember. The upper mounting for the rear damper can also be seen. The axle U-bolts would of course have been painted to match the rest of the chassis.

Those swinging spring shackles were used again at the rear. Only one of the bumperettes is in place here; the four holes through which the other one will be bolted can be seen on the far side of the crossmember.

FACTORY-ORIGINAL WARTIME JEEPS

The machine-gun mount was part of every chassis. Being a Ford chassis, this mounting plate has the script F stamped into it. Willys mounts had a less angular shape. Note that the mount is offset to the right, presumably to counter the weight of the driver.

This general view of the rear of the chassis shows how the damper top mounts were riveted in place. The springs are correctly fitted with U-bolts rather than the clips used on Willys chassis. The dedicated towing mount allowed the rear crossmember to have an open rear face, again saving weight.

Bumperettes were a convenient place to paint unit markings. This one is the right way up, but Jeeps were sometimes seen in service with them mounted upside down, especially if they had been assembled from a crated delivery in a hurry.

A special feature of the Jeeps delivered to Canada from February 1942 was a pair of lifting rings bolted to the front bumper at the top, in line with the dumb-irons. They were attached by screws, nuts and lock-washers.

REAR CROSSMEMBER

The rear crossmember of the chassis frame is a very simple steel pressing with upward tapering outer ends. It is hot-riveted to the top and bottom of each frame side rail and bolted via the pintle or tie plate to the V-section reinforcement for the towing hook. The crossmember is also pre-drilled to take the bumperettes.

Some Jeeps were built with two lifting rings attached to the rear crossmember by screws, nuts and lock-washers. The rings are located within the bumperettes for protection. They were fitted to Jeeps destined for the US Marine Corps and also to those delivered to the Canadian armed forces from February 1942. (Note, however, that while the Canadian vehicles had corresponding rings on the front bumper, the USMC jeeps did not.)

REAR BUMPERETTES

Two bumperettes are bolted to the rear crossmember, to protect the rear of the Jeep against minor collision damage. These bumperettes have their extensions pointing upwards – although it is not uncommon in old pictures to see them pointing the wrong way, especially if the Jeep pictured had been assembled from a crated vehicle.

PINTLE HOOK

The pintle hook is bolted to the A-frame at the rear of the chassis through the pintle or tie plate that joins that frame to the rear crossmember. Willys and Ford used the same basic type of

CHASSIS, SUSPENSION, WHEELS

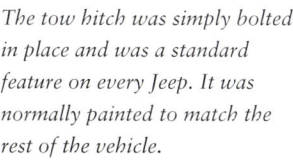

The tow hitch was simply bolted in place and was a standard feature on every Jeep. It was normally painted to match the rest of the vehicle.

The tow hitch is one of very many Jeep items that has been remanufactured and can be bought as a pattern part.

pintle hook, although those associated with each manufacturer actually have several differences. All pintle hooks were painted to match the main body colour.

The one fitted to Willys from the time of the slat-grille models was made by the Holland Hitch Company (then of Holland in Michigan) and its casting is clearly marked "Steel" and with the type designation T60A. At serial number MB 158372 in July 1942, two eye-bolts were added to the pintle hook for the trailer safety chain. During 1945, Willys began to use a different pintle hook that was stamped from steel (rather than cast) and was welded and riveted together. There is some disagreement about when this was introduced, but John Farley has identified the first Willys to have it as MB 431301 in April 1945.

The Ford pintle hook is marked with the type number 60A but has a large script F on the lower jaw, along with the word Ford in script. The safety eye-bolts were probably added at around the same time as on Willys models. However, Ford persisted with the cast pintle hook until the end of production and did not change to a stamped steel type.

CHASSIS NUMBERS

The chassis number of both Willys and Ford Jeeps is found on the left-hand chassis side member at the front. On Willys Jeeps, it is on a small zinc-plated steel plate riveted to the inside of the side member just behind the bumper. On Ford models, it is usually stamped into the top of the frame just behind the shock absorber mounting and the engine mounting bracket, and can be seen from inside the engine bay. However, some Ford chassis have the number stamped further forward, on the top of the frame between the bumper gusset and the radiator support.

On the very early Ford GPW models built on Willys pattern chassis frames, the frame number was stamped into the frame in the standard Ford fashion. The chassis were nevertheless pre-drilled to receive the special rivets of the Willys identification plate, and those two holes remained unused.

Willys used two different types of chassis number plate. Up to June 1944, it was a long narrow plate with curved ends that showed only the chassis number. From June 1944, a larger

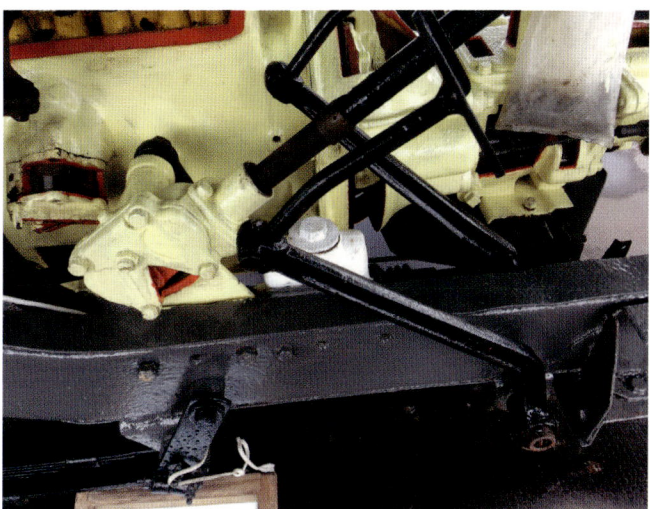

Pictured on the REME instructional chassis are the clutch and brake pedals, mounted on a cross-shaft that passes through brackets welded under the chassis. Note the split pin to hold everything in place. The colours here were intended to aid in training REME mechanics, and are not those used on vehicles in service.

plate was used, describing the vehicle as a Jeep, Willys Scout Car, and showing the chassis number and the address of Willys Overland in Toledo. Early Willys chassis number plates show only the chassis serial number, but later ones incorporated the prefix MB. John Farley has dated the change to February 1942

85

FACTORY-ORIGINAL WARTIME JEEPS

Chassis numbers in position (1): this tag was riveted to the side member just behind the front bumper on a 1942 Willys chassis. It shows the number as being MB186313 and dates the chassis to November that year.

Chassis numbers in position (2): Ford practice was to stamp the chassis number into the top surface of the side-member, just behind the damper mounting on the left-hand side. This one is GPW240374 (the initial letters are very faint), which dates the chassis to December 1944.

and somewhere between chassis numbers 121162 and (MB) 122632. He also notes that from July or early August 1944, a larger gap appeared between the MB prefix letters and the serial number.

Ford used three different types of chassis stamping, but the reasons for the differences and the dates associated with them are not yet clear. The first type has the chassis serial number between two six-pointed stars. The second type is similar but with the letters GPW preceding the first star. The third type begins with the letters GPW, followed by a horizontal double-headed arrow, the serial number, and a second horizontal double-headed arrow.

Chassis numbers and build dates are as shown below. These figures are the ones used by John Farley in *The Standardised War-Time Jeep 2*, and are generally believed to be accurate. However, it is worth noting that they are not the only ones to have been published.

Note, too, that some surviving records are unclear, and that others are incomplete. These figures are therefore as accurate as possible in the present state of collective knowledge about wartime Jeep production. It is also worth remembering that the records on which these figures are based were to some extent theoretical; it is not unknown for a chassis manufactured in a given month to have been used on a later vehicle.

CHASSIS NUMBERS AND BUILD DATES

	WILLYS	FORD		WILLYS	FORD
1941, October	100000 – 100001		1943, October	268891 – 277986	147459 – 155258
1941, November	100002 – 101466		1943, November	277987 – 285516	155259 – 162483
1941, December	101467 – 108172		1943, December	285517 – 293216	162484 – 170019
1942, January	108173 – 115262	1 – 77	1944, January	293217 – 301656	170020 – 177479
1942, February	115263 – 123997	78 – 2195	1944, February	301657 – 309885	177480 – 185020
1942, March	123998 – 132284	2196 – 11115	1944, March	309886 – 318906	185021 – 191013
1942, April	132285 – 139675	11116 – 22274	1944, April	318907 – 327298	191014 – 196563
1942, May	139676 – 148569	22275 – 31198	1944, May	327299 – 338005	196564 – 202557
1942, June	148570 – 155100	31199 – 41960	1944, June	338006 – 347182	202558 – 208329
1942, July	155101 – 163000	41961 – 52355	1944, July	347183 – 356357	208330 – 214101
1942, August	163001 – 173988	52356 – 61156	1944, August	356358 – 366782	214102 – 220095
1942, September	173989 – 177780	61157 – 68842	1944, September	366783 – 375399	220096 – 225867
1942, October	177781 – 185000	68843 – 76050	1944, October	375400 – 383398	225868 – 231822
1942, November	185001 – 192500	76051 – 82118	1944, November	383399 – 393374	231823 – 237701
1942, December	192501 – 199595	82119 – 89378	1944, December	393375 – 403236	247702 – 243416
1943, January	199596 – 207797	89379 – 94705	1945, January	403237 – 412735	243417 – 249547
1943, February	207798 – 215568	94706 – 99719	1945, February	412736 – 421567	248548 – 254873
1943, March	215569 – 222596	99720 – 105230	1945, March	421568 – 431300	254874 – 260809
1943, April	222597 – 231488	105231 – 111167	1945, April	431301 – 438041	260810 – 266011
1943, May	231489 – 237894	111168 – 119416	1945, May	438042 – 445394	266012 – 270306
1943, June	237895 – 246839	119417 – 125441	1945, June	445395 – 451700	270307 – 274383
1943, July	246840 – 252992	125442 – 132184	1945, July	451701 – 454679	274384 – 277873
1943, August	252993 – 260485	132185 – 139606	1945, August	454680 – 459569	
1943, September	260486 – 268890	139607 – 147458	1945, September	459570 – 459875	

CHASSIS, SUSPENSION, WHEELS

The rear shackle for the left-hand front spring was extended in May 1942 to mount a torque reaction spring. The rear end of that auxiliary spring, mounted below the main road spring, is clear in this picture.

The arrangement of the torque reaction spring is seen from the opposite side, in this case on a December 1944 Ford chassis.

ROAD SPRINGS

All four road springs are semi-elliptic types with their leaves made of aluminium alloy. They are mounted above the axles and are located on welded saddles on the axle casings. The front ends of the rear springs and the rear ends of the front springs are bolted to fixed mountings welded to the frame side rails, and their opposite ends are mounted to the frame with U-shaped swinging shackles.

Spring and axle movement is limited by rubber bump-stops mounted under the chassis side rails, and on Ford models the metal mounting plates for these bump-stops are identified with both an F script and a GPW marking.

From the start of MB production in 1941 until 1944, the front springs had eight leaves and the rear springs, which were longer, had nine. Heavy-duty springs were adopted during 1944, with ten leaves at the front and 11 leaves at the rear. No precise changeover point has been identified, and the general agreement is that the new springs were introduced somewhere between June and late 1944. With both the early and late types, left-hand and right-hand springs are identical.

There were of course differences between the Willys springs and those manufactured by Ford. Willys leaf clamps always consisted of a flat metal strap with its ends folded over the top leaf. Ford preferred a U-bolt style of clamp, secured by a bolt (and nut) running across the top surface of the spring.

Two other production changes were recorded. In December 1941 at serial number MB 104726, the spring rebound clips were changed to cover seven leaves instead of six. Then in August 1942 at MB 170307, a spring-shackle lock-bolt was introduced.

Torque reaction spring

The offset engine tended to cause the Jeep to pull left under heavy braking, and the cure was to fit a pair of heavier-duty leaves below the left-hand front spring between its centre and an extension of the shackle for the main spring. This slightly crude (and not 100% effective) solution to the problem was known as a torque reaction spring and was added to Willys models from serial MB 146774 in May 1942. Ford models followed suit from about mid-July. This auxiliary spring could also be fitted retrospectively to earlier Jeeps.

DAMPERS (SHOCK ABSORBERS)

A telescopic shock absorber is fitted at each wheel station. Willys always used Monroe items, and from December 1942 switched to a refillable Monroe shock absorber; soon after

The Ford script logo was even stamped into the top mountings for the front dampers. This is the late 1944 chassis again.

The arrangement of the steering arm, front damper, and brake flexible hose is clear in this close-up of a 1942 model.

Most Jeeps had this steering arrangement, with the right and left tie rods both attached to the drag link. Note the clamps on the ends of the tie-rods.

The steering arrangement is seen here in more detail on the REME instructional chassis.

that the head of the damper changed from spot-welded to seam-welded. Ford, by contrast, always used non-refillable Gabriel shock absorbers, and branded these with their usual script F.

STEERING

It hardly needs saying that all Jeeps were built with left-hand drive; no right-hand drive models were ever manufactured. All of them have a broadly similar steering system, with a variable-ratio cam and lever steering box giving ratios of between 12:1 (at the straight-ahead) and 14:1 (on full lock). The steering box is bolted to the left-hand side rail of the frame, and its drop arm is bolted to a short drag link which leads to a bellcrank mounted on top of the front axle. The forward end of the bell crank is then connected to each front hub by means of a track rod.

Willys used a steering box made by Ross from the start of production. There were minor differences between the type used on slat-grille models and those used after February 1942, but all steering boxes have the Ross name cast into their outer casings. Ford used a similar steering box made in their own factories, which is readily identifiable by F script and GPW markings on the casing.

Willys steering arms are marked TP, and have a spring and cup washer. The Ford steering arms are marked with a script F, and have a felt seal around the shaft, plus a cup washer.

One early production change was recorded, and in December 1941 at serial number MB 103317, four of the 16 steering arm studs on slat-grille models were changed from straight to dowel studs.

The steering box was always a simple Ross type with a variable ratio or a Ford version of it, and was bolted to the left-hand chassis rail.

CHASSIS, SUSPENSION, WHEELS

Painted white for training purposes, this is the brake master cylinder on the REME instructional chassis.

Again seen on the instructional chassis, this cutaway shows the layout of a front brake and front hub, in this case on the left-hand side.

BRAKES

Both Willys and Ford Jeeps have twin-shoe drum brakes on all four wheels, with hydraulic actuation. The shoes have a leading-and-trailing arrangement. The drums are 9 inches in diameter and 1¾in wide, and were made by Kelsey-Hayes; they can be turned to a maximum of .030in oversize. Brake drums of Chevrolet manufacture have also been found, but these are generally thought to have been motor pool replacements. All drums were painted Olive Drab.

The operating mechanism was made by Bendix, and the hydraulic system by Lockheed. The wheel cylinders have a 1-inch diameter on the front wheels and (on early models) a 7/8in diameter on the rear wheels. The brake master cylinder has a 1-inch diameter, incorporates the fluid reservoir and is mounted to the left-hand chassis rail. It is painted Olive Drab.

There were some changes to the braking system during slat-grille production, in December 1941. At serial number MB 106764, the rear brake hose was re-routed from a bracket on the inner face of the left-hand side rail to run along the crossmember ahead of the rear axle. At the same time, the brake pipes on the left-hand side of the rear axle and between the master cylinder and the hose also changed. John Farley suggests that the redundant bracket may have remained on some chassis after the other changes had been made. A further change was made to the rear wheel cylinders at MB 134356 in April 1942. Originally 7/8in in diameter, they were changed to a ¾-inch diameter.

The parking brake (emergency brake) acts on the rear transmission output shaft on all production models, and not on the wheels. In the beginning, the brake was an external contracting type (ie with the brake shoes on the outside). However, on Willys models from September 1944 this was replaced by an internal expanding type (ie with the shoes on the inside of the drum, like a conventional wheel brake). This change took place at MB 37337 and brought with it some other modifications because the new parking brake was physically larger than the one it replaced. Ford models retained the original type of parking brake throughout production.

The layout of the rear brake and rear hub is seen here.

Looking a little forlorn with no lever attached, this was the linkage for the transmission brake.

Front axles, in this case on a 1942 Ford GPW, were helpfully marked as such.

Neatly painted up for clarity, this is the rear differential on the instructional chassis.

Pictured on a 1942 slat-grille model, this is an example of the early "solid" steel disc wheel, without the split-rim feature introduced later.

AXLES AND DIFFERENTIALS

All Jeep MB and GPW axles were Spicer fully floating types, with hypoid bevel gears in the differential. Rear axles have half-shafts with splines at the inner ends and bolt to the hubs at the outer end. Front axles have fully enclosed constant-velocity joints (made by several different manufacturers) and again bolt to the hub flange. Their steering knuckles use roller bearings. All differentials have a 4.88:1 gearset.

Nevertheless, there are differences between the Willys and the Ford axles. The Willys axles have a "W" for Willys and the number 16378 cast on the axle web. On the differential cover plate, the instruction "Use Hypoid Oil Only" is cast into the surface below the filler plug, and on the other side of the cover is cast "W 16977".

The Ford axles have "GP 3075" cast on the front axle flange, and "GP 4025" cast on the rear axle flange. They have the same "Use Hypoid Oil Only" instruction cast into the surface of the cover plate below the filler plug. On the inside of the cover plate is cast "GP 4016", accompanied by the Ford script "F". Ford axles also changed from a cast differential cover plate to a stamped type, probably in the first half of 1944. Willys axles nevertheless retained their original cast type of cover.

WHEELS

The wheels on all MB Jeeps are plain disc types, with a five-bolt fixing pattern, a 16-inch diameter and a 4-inch rim width. The threads of the securing bolts are handed, so that there is a right-hand thread on the right of the vehicle and a left-hand thread on the left of the vehicle. This arrangement was adopted because it allowed the normal rotation of the wheels to tighten the nuts rather than to loosen them. The studs are normally stamped with an R or an L at the end, and the nuts are also marked. Right-hand thread nuts have either three Rs or no marking at all, while left-hand thread nuts have three Ls or small notches around their edges.

There were two major types of wheel. Early Willys Jeeps had one-piece disc wheels, often described as "solid" types because they have no ventilation slots. Later Willys and all Ford models were built with split-rim "combat" wheels.

Willys Jeeps were fitted with solid wheels up to February 1942. These are stamped with various markings towards the outer edge of the face, across from the hole for the valve stem. Although there are variations in the way the markings are stamped, all markings include "16 x 4.00" and a date of manufacture, typically expressed as "43 2" (for February 1943); the date stamps are rarely in a straight line! Some wheels also have a maker's code or logo as well. A few early Willys Jeeps did have 4.5-inch rims, but a check of the date stamp will reveal whether these are likely to be genuine or are the 4.5-inch size of very similar appearance that was used on post-war civilian Jeeps.

Ford Jeeps had split-rim combat wheels from the start of production in January 1942, and these were also fitted on

CHASSIS, SUSPENSION, WHEELS

This is the later split-rim wheel, with the domed heads of its fixing bolts clearly visible around the well of the rim.

production to Willys Jeeps from serial number 120700 in February 1942. The split-rim wheels were manufactured by Kelsey-Hayes in Akron, Ohio, and are readily identifiable by the eight domed bolt heads visible in their outer faces. These wheels also had a warning tag welded to the outer face, stressing that the tyre should be deflated before the rim nuts were removed. The split-rim wheels are marked with the Kelsey-Hayes name, the rim size and a date of manufacture. Interestingly, Ford did not add its own F script to the ones it fitted to GPW models. These wheels all have a bead retainer around the well of the rim and were originally fitted with Schrader valve-stem protectors.

TYRES

The standard tyres on all Jeeps were 6.00 x 16 size with a heavy-duty six-ply construction, although a small number of early Willys Jeeps with 4.5-inch wheel rims had 6.50 x 16 tyres. The tyres were known as NDT types, those letters standing for Non-Directional Tread; they are more familiarly known as bar grip types. These tyres always had separate inner tubes, and the recommended tyre pressures were 30psi on the front wheels and 35psi on the rears.

Several makes of tyre were fitted on the Willys production lines, including Goodyear. Ford made its own tyres at the Dearborn plant during 1942, but in December that year the US Government bought the whole tyre and inner tube manufacturing facility. It dismantled this and shipped it to Russia in support of its then-ally, but the probability is that the plant was never reassembled at its destination. Ford then turned to Firestone for its supplies of Jeep tyres until production ended in 1945.

The rear hubs had indentations around their rims on most MB and GPW Jeeps. This hub on a 1945 Ford is typical.

ADDITIONS

There was an almost infinite number of unit or motor pool modifications to the Jeep in wartime. The vehicle was always intended to be adaptable, and some of the adaptations probably exceeded even the wildest fantasies of its original creators. Nevertheless, some standardised modifications were authorised by the US QMC, and there were also several items of onboard kit supplied by the Jeep factories that have not been discussed in the earlier sections of this book. All of these are therefore scooped up together in this final section. They are listed alphabetically for ease of reference.

AIRPORTABLE MODIFICATIONS

When Jeeps were transported in aircraft that had not originally been designed to carry them, some modifications had to be made. Both the C-47 Dakota transport and the Horsa glider were loaded through a side door which made it necessary to turn a Jeep through a 90-degree angle to get it into the fuselage. In order to achieve that, the front bumper ends of the Jeep had to be cut back to the chassis rails, and sometimes the spare wheel and the jerrycan would also be removed – although not permanently. The spare wheel could of course be relocated between the chassis rails ahead of the radiator grille. Jeeps used in airporting operations sometimes had a large stowage basket fitted at the rear – but this was usually removed to aid loading into the aircraft.

It was also important to reduce the vehicle's height. In some cases, the top section of the steering wheel would be cut away so that it did not stand up above the top of the dash; in other cases, the same end was achieved by adapting the steering wheel securing nut so that the wheel could be quickly removed and refitted; some steering wheels were even modified with a hinged section.

CAPSTAN WINCH

From 1945, Jeeps could be fitted with a front-mounted capstan winch, and the winch could of course also be fitted retrospectively to earlier vehicles. Its purpose was for self-recovery if the vehicle became trapped in mud, or for assisting in the recovery of another vehicle.

The winch itself was a Braden J2 type, which was also used on other US military vehicles of the time. It was mounted to a dedicated plate that sat between the grille and the front bumper and was bolted to the chassis rail on either side. Fitting required a modified steering bell crank that lowered the track rods to give clearance for the underside of the winch assembly. The winch was driven by a propshaft running to an adaptor on

The Braden capstan winch was available for units to fit and had its own mounting plate that bolted between the front ends of the chassis rails.

Control lever and operating instructions plate for the Braden winch.

ADDITIONS

the starter dog. With the engine running and the gearbox in neutral, power was engaged through a clutch mechanism on the winch itself. The recommended engine speed for winching was 1200rpm, and the winch was capable of a maximum 5000 lb pull.

The correct wartime version of this winch has four cap screws in the capstan head, and has a metal plate with operating instructions alongside the winch engagement lever, which has a black ball-type grip. Note that the post-war version of this winch, which was available for the CJ-2A civilian Jeep, has some differences. Braden winches have a seven-digit serial number, of which the first two digits indicate the year of manufacture.

DECONTAMINATOR

Many Jeeps carried decontaminator units in the field. The decontaminator was designed to neutralise the toxic chemicals (such as mustard gas) that might be encountered during warfare, and looked rather like a fire extinguisher. For that reason it was clearly labelled as not to be used for extinguishing fires. When first fitted, it was typically mounted to the sloping rear face of the driver's side wing (fender) on a bracket similar to the single-strap type of fire extinguisher bracket. Late Type 2 composite body tubs were fitted at the factory with mounting holes and captive fixing nuts in the floor behind the passenger's seat, where the bracket was normally mounted. These fixings were probably first added in early 1945.

The standard decontaminator was an M2 type. It consisted of a brass cylinder about 18 inches long and 3 inches in diameter, with a T-shaped operating handle on the top. The unit was refillable through a screw cap, and in fact had to be refilled every three months because the contents lost their effectiveness over time. The filling was typically a chemical called DANC (Decontaminating Agent, Non-Corrosive), which in spite of its name tended to cause rapid corrosion of the brass parts of the decontaminator. Units typically had a brass identification plate around the upper section of the cylinder, with a very slight relief for the lettering. Some appear to have had decal labels.

One filling of the decontaminator would tackle up to 12 square yards of contaminated surface and was enough for about 90 seconds of discharge. The M2 Decontaminator could project its contents as a spray up to about five feet. Four different manufacturers are known: Badger, Buffalo, Fyr Fyter and General Detroit.

FIRE EXTINGUISHER

On the earliest Jeeps, a fire extinguisher was mounted in a bracket on the passenger's side of the dash, but from February 1942 (when the glove box was introduced) it was moved to the side wall of the driver's footwell. The new fixings for this later fitting were visible on the outside of the scuttle panel.

There was a further change to the mounting bracket late in 1943. Early brackets had a bowl-type mounting at the foot and a single strap and clip near the top. A second strap and clip were added near the foot on the later brackets, and the bowl was simplified.

On early Jeeps, the fire extinguisher had a polished brass body, but from June 1942 it was normally finished in Olive Drab, presumably to avoid unwelcome reflections. Several different suppliers provided the extinguishers fitted to MB and GPW Jeeps, and all extinguishers had a capacity of one quart. Among the types of extinguisher believed to have been supplied as original equipment are these:

The fire extinguisher was mounted in the driver's footwell from early 1942. The extinguisher itself is a Pyrene type and the bracket is the later two-strap type. As this is a 1945 model, the extinguisher would probably originally have been painted in Olive Drab rather than polished, as here.

Fire Gun   type 0
  (made by American LaFrance Foamite Company)
Fyr-Fyter   type D-10A
Pyrene   Heavy Vehicle Type
  (made by the Extinguisher and Chemical Company)
SOS Fire Guard   model 85
  (made by the General Detroit Corporation)

A Jeep with everything.... this one has a pedestal machine-gun mount carrying a .50 cal machine gun, and a vertical holder for two rifles in front of it.

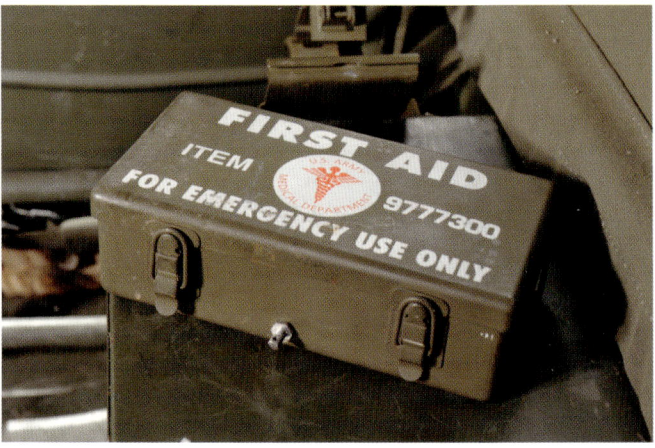

This is a post-March 1944 First Aid kit; earlier ones had different markings. The metal fitting at the front lower edge is not original.

FIRST AID KIT

A First Aid Kit became part of the standard Jeep specification from June 1944. This has a metal case with four clip-type catches, and is marked For Emergency Use Only. (The cases of earlier kits had different markings, and some had hinges.) This kit contained the following items, many in clearly labelled paper packets:

    16 adhesive white gauze bandages (1in x 3in)
    burn injury set with boric acid ointment
    card with safety pins
    eye dressing set
    four white gauze compresses (2in x 2in)
    packet of 10 aromatic ammonia ampoules
    packet of 10 iodine swabs
    set of tourniquet, scissors and forceps.
    triangular white compress badage
    white gauze compress (4in x 4in)
    white gauze bandage (4in x 6 yards).

GUN MOUNTS

The gun mount fitted as standard to the Jeep's chassis frame was designed to accept the US Army's M31 machine gun pedestal, which had triple bracing. An improved M31C type followed in 1945, but too late to see much combat use during the war. Units in the field inevitably created their own pedestal mounts and adapted other types as well. The weapons most commonly used on the M31 mount were the .30 cal and .50 cal machine guns.

A scuttle-mounted gun support was also introduced in 1943, and was known as the M48 bracket mount. This allowed a .30 cal machine gun or .30 cal Browning automatic rifle to be mounted ahead of the passenger's seat, firing forwards. Again, troops in the field often developed their own improvised equivalents.

ADDITIONS

This is the late type of standardised aerial mounting bracket. The base of the aerial is protected by a cover.

RADIO EQUIPMENT

Jeeps could be equipped with either six-volt or 12-volt radio sets. The 12-volt types needed additional modifications to the electrical system. Radios were installed by the user arm but radio Jeeps were modified using standard installation kits.

Note that there is a wealth of information about US Second World War radios available online, and some aspects of the subject are still controversial. It is advisable to investigate very closely before either buying a set of equipment or installing it.

Aerial

Jeeps equipped with a radio normally carried a long whip aerial that was mounted on a bracket bolted to the upper left-hand side of the rear body tub, between the wheel arch and the corner lifting handle. This bracket had part number MP-50. The base of the antenna had part number MP-48 and was made of porcelain by Ohio Brass and branded with that company's name. Aerials typically ran forwards and were secured over the front of the Jeep by a cable or wire to a suitable point on the body.

Although this arrangement was recommended, it was far from invariable. There were undoubtedly variations in the mounting position and even in the mounting bracket to suit requirements in the field.

The aerial mounting bracket is different here, but the base of the aerial is clear. The main "whip" aerial would have been mounted to the top of it and, typically, pulled forwards in an arc and secured to the body somewhere near the front.

95

One way of obtaining 12 volts to run radios was to use a generator mounted between the seats and driven from the power take-off. It was concealed under a metal cover with cooling louvres to allow air to circulate.

AUXILIARY GENERATOR, 12-VOLT

Some Jeeps were fitted with a 12-volt, 55-amp auxiliary generator that was driven by a vee-belt from the power take-off on the back of the transfer box and was mounted to the floor between the front seats. This was certainly available by May 1943 and possibly earlier, but could of course be fitted to Jeeps of any age in the field.

The generator was protected by a curved metal cover. It had its own regulator and charged a pair of six-volt batteries, installed one behind each front seat. The power supplied to the radio was independent of the vehicle's own electrical system.

The 12-volt regulator box used with the engine-mounted 12-volt generator had a green label. This is the correct type of box – although in this case it is supporting a complete conversion to more modern 12-volt electrics!

This instruction plate probably had a black background to make it easier to read when it was new, but years of honest wear have not diminished its ability to provide guidance on how to charge the radio batteries.

This system was typically (but not invariably) used with radio set SCR-193-KB. A total of 1000 kits was supposedly manufactured.

Ford also developed their own 12-volt electrical installation, which was somewhat simpler. This was typically used with radio set SCR-193-K. A 12-volt 55-amp Autolite generator (type AL GDJ-4808) replaced the six-volt type on the engine, and the standard voltage regulator box was replaced by a 12-volt Autolite type (type AL-VRH-4101C, with a green rather than red data plate). A longer fan belt was also needed. The system depended on two six-volt batteries connected in series and installed between the front seats. These batteries powered both the vehicle's own electrical system and the radio set. This conversion was available by May 1944 and a total of 2500 kits is thought to have been manufactured.

RADIO OUTLET BOX

From March 1943, Jeeps were fitted with the basic requirements for radio equipment in the factories as a matter of course. A radio outlet box was attached to the inside of the rear body alongside the passenger seat by means of four bolts that passed through the side of the body. The body itself had four elongated holes to receive these and to give a little leeway in the mounting position. Willys used four hexagon-head bolts with one plain washer and one lead washer on the outside, and a lock washer and nut on the inside of the box itself. Ford used roundhead slotted machine screws and washers.

The box itself contains a filter and a terminal block. It has an elbow and a conduit at one end, and a grommet on top at the other end where the radio cable enters. The conduit passes through the floorpan and on to the starting switch. A hole in the floor pan allows the earth cable to pass through and to run under the floor pan before being attached to the chassis frame.

The radio junction box was bolted through the body side at four points. Seen here are the elongated holes that gave a little leeway in its positioning.

RADIO SETS

Radio equipment was typically mounted on the wheelbox behind the driver, with the controls facing the centre of the vehicle. In some cases (including in British use), it was mounted on a platform or table in the rear of the vehicle that occupied the space where the rear seat was normally located.

The US Army typically used a radio made by the Galvin Manufacturing Corporation of Chicago, but other allies fitted their own sets. Typically (but by no means invariably), the radio used in a US Army Jeep would be a Galvin BC-659 set, contained in metal boxes with clamped lids and leather suitcase-type handles. Among the 12-volt radio sets used were the SCR-193-K and SCR-193-KB.

Radio suppression system

Jeeps were fitted with radio suppression equipment of two types. The Type 1 suppression equipment consisted of a filterette bolted to the engine side of the bulkhead (firewall), and this was used on production from the beginning until approximately March 1943. There was then a change to Type 2 radio suppression equipment, which was achieved through a radio junction box fitted inside the body.

The US Army favoured Galvin radio sets, although several different types were fitted. This one is a BC-620-A set.

Another Galvin radio in a US Jeep, this time the more common BC-659-J type.

depended on which supplier served the factory where the vehicle was assembled.

The filterette is regularly omitted (or disconnected) on enthusiast vehicles today because its only value is to improve radio reception, which does not affect the everyday usability of the Jeep.

Type 2 (radio junction box)

From March 1943, Jeeps were fitted as standard with a radio junction box that was located on the inside of the body between the passenger seat and the body side. The first Willys model so fitted was MB 217543. Some experts believe that there was a production overlap between the Type 1 and Type 2 suppression systems, with the result that some Jeeps built in mid-1943 had both a filterette and a radio junction box.

The radio junction box is normally tinned and then painted Olive Drab. It is secured through the body side by four hex-head bolts on Willys models and by four slotted, round-head, machine-thread screws on Ford types. The heads of the fixings and their washers are visible on the outside of the body, just ahead of the right-hand rear wheel. The fixing holes in the body side were elongated to allow some tolerance in the fixing position.

The Type 2 suppression system also affected other areas of the vehicle, where external bonding washers were fitted; there was also an earth cable between the rear bolt of the generator and the starter bracket and to the rear bolt of the front engine mounting.

The suppression system was improved with additional filters and earth straps in late 1943, and a kit produced by the US Signal Corps provided additional shielding for the coil, distributor, ignition leads and spark plugs.

RIFLE RACK

A fairly common field modification was to fit a vertical rifle rack, either outboard of the driver or between the front seats.

SPARE PARTS BAG

Each Jeep left the factory with a spare parts bag, which contained a spark plug, bulbs, cotter pins, fan belt, valve cores, tyre, inner tube and wheel.

SURGE TANK

A surge tank was developed for hot-weather (typically desert) conditions and has the same function as a modern radiator overflow tank. The kit was designed to be fitted in the field, and consisted of the tank, a tank cap, a tank shield, hoses and mounting brackets. The impetus for its introduction is thought to have come from British use of Jeeps in North Africa in 1942.

The surge tank itself is mounted vertically and bolted by brackets to the first two grille slats on the right (passenger's side) of the vehicle. It is supplied with an unpressured cap, which has to be exchanged with the radiator pressure cap; the

Type 1 (filterette)

There were four holes in the bulkhead (firewall) to which the filterette was fitted. Willys initially used a filterette made by Tobe-Deutschmann (whose factory was in Canton, Massachusetts), and in April 1942 changed to one made by Mallory (of Indianapolis). The theoretical changeover point was at serial number MB 137916, but it seems probable that the changeover was actually more gradual than this suggests.

The early Ford filterette was again a Tobe-Deutschmann type, but there was a change (probably in early 1942) to a Sprague 18960, which was of course adorned with an F script marking. From September 1942 a type 18960-B was listed, and then in the early part of 1943 Ford used filters made by Tobe-Deutschmann, Solar, and Mallory. The type fitted probably

ADDITIONS

The surge tank was normally fitted to Jeeps operating in hot-climate conditions. This is the basic tank, seen here without its protective shield.

A rear tonneau cover was available, and is seen here in place on a slat-grille Willys.

pressure cap is then fitted to the surge tank. The tubing for the surge tank is tapped into the radiator overflow tubing, and the saddle-type shield is then fitted over the tank, being bolted through the edge of the grille panel and to a grille slat by clamp brackets on the other side.

TONNEAU COVER

Among the options available was a tonneau cover for the rear of the body. Mainly used to protect valuable items from inclement weather, it was not particularly common.

TOW ROPE

Most Jeeps carried a tow rope. This was often wound around the front bumper, mainly to avoid using up valuable space within the body.

... and this is the tank with the protective shield in place. In this case, there is a discrepancy between the finish of the shield and the paint on the Jeep!

Tow ropes were often wrapped around the front bumper. There was no "approved" way of doing it, and this is as authentic as any. The Dutch civilian number-plate would of course not have been present!

Jeep trailers were manufactured by Bantam and Willys, and had a quarter-ton cargo payload.

TRAILERS

A special quarter-ton cargo trailer was developed for use with the Jeep and was built in quantity by Willys and by Bantam. The design was very distinctive, with flared tops at the sides over two wheels with cycle-type mudguards. The Bantam type was known as the T3, and 73,569 examples were built during the war. The Willys type was known as the MBT and a total of 59,956 were built. A further 9843 trailers were built to the same design by ten smaller companies, making a grand total of 143,368. All these trailers had a triangular drawbar and a loop-type hitch, but many surviving examples have been modified to suit civilian-type 2-inch or 50mm ball-type hitches.

TYRE OPTIONS

Jeeps in desert service were sometimes fitted with 7.50 x 16 NDT tyres to improve traction in sand. This option may not have been introduced before April 1943.

VEHICLE TOOLS

Jeeps were supplied from new with a comprehensive tool kit that enabled users to carry out emergency maintenance tasks in the field; obviously, regular maintenance was the primary responsibility of the motor pools.

The Jeep's on-board tool kit consisted of the items listed below. Most of the tools supplied by Ford were branded with the Ford logo.

- 16oz ball-peen hammer
- Electrical tape (half-pound roll)
- Grease gun (lubricating gun)
- Hub puller
- Jack
- Padlocks (two)
- Selection of spanners (wrenches)
- Selection of screwdrivers
- Starting handle (normally stowed behind the rear seat)
- Tyre pump (normally stowed under the rear seat)
- Tyre chains
- Wheel brace

There has been considerable debate about the exact types of some of these tools. Tyre pumps, for example, have been found in black, grey, green and Olive Drab, and with either no branding or branded as manufactured by Dalton Foundries or Walker. The grease gun is generally thought to have been either an Alemite 6593 lever-operated type or one manufactured by Lincoln.

ADDITIONS

The Westinghouse air compressor is seen here, with its additional drive belt leading from a double pulley on the crankshaft nose.

WATERPROOFING

Although Jeeps had a basic level of waterproofing, they were not prepared for deep-water wading as standard. An appliqué waterproofing kit was developed before the D-Day landings, its main disadvantage being that it took a long time to fit.

WESTINGHOUSE AIR COMPRESSOR

Jeeps used in conditions where it was necessary to deflate and re-inflate tyres – such as in soft desert sand or snow – could be

This type of additional locker was associated with the air compressor kit, and was probably normally used to stow the air hose. In this case, the hasp has been fitted with a padlock to deter thieves. The green fire extinguisher visible under the dash is not original but is a sensible modern precaution.

fitted with an engine-driven air compressor. A kit for the purpose was introduced probably in October 1944.

The compressor itself was a Westinghouse T1 type that was also used on Chevrolet and GMC military trucks of the time. Its fitting kit consisted of brackets to mount the compressor to the top left of the engine, a double crankshaft pulley, an additional rubber drive belt, and a long detachable black rubber air hose. This could be stowed in a lidded pannier that fitted behind the right-hand front wing and appears to have been part of the kit.

Battered, perhaps, but the instruction plate on the air compressor is still just about legible.

FACTORY-ORIGINAL WARTIME JEEPS

Pictured in preservation, this Jeep has another variety of side canvas and is fitted with a wire-cutter mounted on the front bumper.

WIRE-CUTTER

There was no standard specification for the wire-cutter, which probably first appeared on Jeeps in North Africa during 1943. Communications wires strung over roads could drop to a level where they would cause injury to the occupants of Jeeps, and it was not long before it became a deliberate enemy tactic to stretch wire across roads at head height. The wire cutter was therefore developed to deal with this threat.

Wire cutters were mounted to the front bumper of a Jeep to cut the wire before it reached the vehicle's occupants. Typically, the wire-cutter itself might be no more than a piece of angle-iron, fitted by units in the field and braced to the front of the vehicle. Some more sophisticated variants incorporated a notch that was designed to trap the wire and break it

APPENDIX A
BRITISH JEEPS

The main purpose of this Appendix is to give an idea of the modifications made by the British military, which are less well known than those made by the US Forces but were no less "authentic". British enthusiasts restoring a vehicle may wish to check this Appendix before removing an item that seems not to be authentic for a US Jeep! The lists here may also help in determining the original purpose of a seemingly non-standard bracket or bolt hole on a Jeep believed once to have been in British service.

The British military was the largest users of Jeeps outside the US Forces, and contract records show that around 41,000 were delivered directly, of which 10,000 were reconditioned examples. Nevertheless, the full total was over 105,000 (including GPA amphibians), as large quantities were supplied directly by the US Army. The next largest user was the Soviet Union, with a total of just under 53,000, including GPA models. The British Jeeps were supplied under the Anglo-American Mutual Aid Agreement of February 1942. This was a wide-ranging agreement between Britain and the USA to provide one another with equipment, services and other assistance without charging commercial payments.

The first Jeeps were supplied to Britain in 1941 and were Bantam 40BRC types; a further 150 Bantams were supplied in 1943, and there were also 270 examples of the Ford GP in 1941. However, the bulk of the British Jeeps were Willys MB or Ford GPW types. In 1942-1943, there were also a few hundred amphibious Ford GPA models, although different authorities quote different totals of between 380 and 852!

IDENTIFICATION

The details of the Ministry of Supply contracts for standardised Jeeps are as follows. These tables are derived from those in Pat Ware's book, *Quarter-Ton*. They show the British WD registrations of each batch of vehicles.

Contract SM 2275 (1941) — 32,791 vehicles

Willys MB	21,291 vehicles	M4768471-4771580
		M5220001-5221200
		M5534138-5539697
Willys MB (recon)	5000 vehicles	M6128340-6133339
Ford GPW	1500 vehicles	M5473073-5475927
		M5557518-5558171
		M5571048-5572845
		M5583414-5584413
		M5825890-5827389
		M5833457-5834956
		M5844127-5845740
		M6181796-6183795
		M6269725-6270724
Ford GPW (recon)	5000 vehicles	M6133340-6138339

Note: Although the figures for reconditioned vehicles were quoted as 5000 of each major type, it is highly unlikely that the split between MB and GPW was as exact as this suggests.

Contract SM 2428 (1942) — 2000 vehicles
Willys MB — M4922197-4923996

Contract W398-QM-11423 (1942)
Contract W398-QM-11424 (1942) — 4043 vehicles
MB and GPW
M4938020-4939019
M4940655
M4957976-4958017
M5155534-5158533

Note: These vehicles were supplied directly to the War Department without a separate Ministry of Supply contract. They had originally been destined for the US Army and had already been allocated US hood numbers. These were 2073506-2978606 (first contract) and 20100000-20163145 (second contract). In many cases, the US numbers were simply painted over and a new British number was applied.

Contract SM 2402 (1943) — 185 vehicles
Willys MB (See note below)
Note: These vehicles were supplied to New Zealand. They may have been registered in a series that included M1332213-1332279.

Contract BM5485 (1944) — 1500 vehicles
Willys MB — 1407 vehicles
Ford GPW — 93 vehicles — M5558376-5559875
Note: These vehicles were described as "ex-US Forces".

Contract SM6047 (1945) — 4 vehicles
Willys MB-L

(Numbers probably not allocated; the MB-L was an experimental lightweight version of the Jeep)

Although large numbers of Jeeps were cast shortly after the end of the war, a good number remained in British service. Those still in service at the time of the 1949 census, when a new military registration number system was introduced, were allocated numbers in the series 00 YH 01 to 99 YH 99 and 00 YJ 01 to 99 YJ 99. A 1954 War Department document noted that 8750 Jeeps were still on strength at that stage, although around 2500 were unserviceable.

Jeeps were supplied to Britain in crated form, each one in its own packing case. They were partially stripped down for packing to save space, and the elements that had been removed were shipped in the same crate as the Jeep. They were then reassembled on arrival in Britain, tested, marked with a registration number and sent to a storage depot from where they would be issued to their end users.

FEATURES OF BRITISH JEEPS

British Construction and Use Regulations required certain modifications to the Jeeps, and so did the British military. As a result, British Jeeps had a number of differences from their American counterparts. These differences were set out in a

Slat-grille M4768471 was the very first British Jeep, delivered under contract SM 2275 in May 1942. (Imperial War Museum)

This 1942 slat-grille Jeep belonged to the British 1st Airborne Division, and its steering wheel has been cut away at the top to suit air porting operations. (Imperial War Museum/ WikiMedia Commons)

drawing dated 28 July 1942, which was later re-issued with minor changes. It is not clear whether all the modifications incorporated in the drawing were fitted to all British Jeeps, and one modification (a bracket attached to the spare wheel) appears never to have been fitted at all. The modifications were made when the Jeeps arrived in Britain, and not at the factory of origin.

The British modifications were as follows.

Body and fittings

From July 1942, Jeeps used by British forces were fitted with open stowage panniers that were bolted to the sloping rear face of each front wing. These panniers had footman loops and straps, and were commonly used to carry a square 2-gallon fuel can, but were subsequently modified to take the standard 20-litre jerrycan. They were not generally fitted after the rear jerrycan holder became standard on new Jeeps in March 1943.

Rifle clips were fitted to the outside (not the inside) of the windscreen panel, between July 1942 and September 1943, when a standardised type of rifle holder was fitted from the factories. British Jeeps sometimes carried a British spade, distinguished from its American equivalent by a T-handle instead of a D-handle.

British Jeeps used in the Middle East theatre were painted Matt Sand over the standard Olive Drab that came from the factory. Those Jeeps retained after the war were mainly repainted in the standard "peacetime" colour of Deep Bronze Green.

Lighting and electrics

The standard Jeep lighting system did not meet British Construction and Use regulations, and as a result large numbers were modified. The modifications nevertheless appear not to have been made to all British Jeeps. They were made to those vehicles that were operated in Britain, but those destined for service in other theatres (and not used at home) often escaped modification to save time and costs.

The "home" Jeeps had their front blackout lights relocated from the grille panel to the tops of the front wings. These lights were also rewired to act as sidelamps. The passenger's side headlamp was replaced by a yellow bridge plate, and the driver's side headlamp was often replaced by a Butler type, which on "home" Jeeps typically had a blackout mask added to it. In such cases, it appears that the standard blackout driving lamp was removed from the driver's side wing.

At the rear, the standard tail lights were sometimes replaced by British-made Lucas units (probably mainly to simplify spares logistics), and on Jeeps delivered without a trailer socket, a standard British trailer socket was added. Another special British feature was a convoy light at the rear, which was probably first fitted in July 1942. This was mounted on a special bracket on the rear cross-member and shone under the vehicle to illuminate a white-painted area

This early British Jeep posed for an official photograph is a "script" Willys, and shows the wing-mounted fuel can holder. This one was almost certainly designed to take the standard British two-gallon "square" fuel can. (Imperial War Museum)

on the rear differential; in blackout conditions, this allowed a following driver to gauge where the vehicle was but could not be seen from the air. The light was operated by a switch mounted low down on the tail panel (for example, just above the right-hand bumperette).

Post-war, some Jeeps were converted to a 24-volt electrical system so that they could operate with more modern military radios. These vehicles were also fitted with a pair of additional batteries in the rear compartment. The extra batteries were for the radio only and were not connected to the vehicle's main electrical system.

Dash and interior

A common British modification was to bolt a 400mm ammunition box to the floor between the two front seats, where it could serve for stowage of any number of different items. Further arrangements for extra stowage were made at the rear, where footman loops were added to the inside of the body on the right-hand side, and were provided with straps.

The British military modified the uprights of the rear seat backrest so that this could be more easily removed. They sometimes also modified the seat cushion and the tray in which it was carried, so that these could be removed easily by using turnbuckles. Another British modification in this area was the addition of footman loops to the right-hand inner body panel, which held straps for additional stowage.

The soldier's helmet and the Jeep are both unmistakeably British. The left-hand headlamp aperture is obscured by a bridge plate, there is a blackout lamp in the right-hand aperture, and the small blackout lamps have been relocated to the tops of the wings. This Jeep belonged to the 11th Armoured Division and was pictured in October 1944. (Imperial War Museum/ WikiMedia Commons)

Engine
British Jeeps ran throughout the war with the original type of Carter carburettor, but those that remained in service during the 1950s were sometimes fitted with a Solex 32 PB-2 type, similar to the Solex M32 PBIC built in France for the Hotchkiss M201 derivative of the Jeep.

Those Jeeps that remained in British service after the war generally had their engines repainted in the standard British engine colour of Duck Egg Blue.

Radio equipment
In wartime use, radio-equipped British Jeeps would typically have had the no 19, no 22 or no 37 W/T sets.

After the war, Jeeps still in service that were adapted for radio work had the Larkspur system. The Larkspur radio set itself was mounted on a carrier that fitted across the back of the body in place of the rear seat. The batteries were carried underneath this. An aerial tuner bracket was fitted to a sheet-metal bracket on the top of one of the front wings; the tuner box would be mounted above this, with the aerial in turn on top of it. The headset adapter was fitted to the dash, to the right of the handbrake where it could be reached by the front passenger.

Some British modifications
The Jeep was always intended to be adaptable, and it would be impossible to list all the uses that user units found for it. However, it is worth highlighting some of the modifications and adaptations made in British service.

Light recovery vehicles
Some units modified Jeeps in the field to act as light recovery vehicles. The usual method was to fabricate a simple A-frame jib from angle-iron and to mount it in the rear of the body with a hand winch and appropriate cabling. Some small garage businesses made similar modifications to surplus Jeeps after the war, and some may even have used genuine unit-converted examples.

Linelayers
Some Jeeps were modified to act as linelayers for the Royal Corps of Signals. Typically, the windscreen would be removed

altogether and the spare wheel would be carried on the bonnet. The reels of cable would then be mounted on special brackets at the front and the rear that allowed the cable to be paid out as the vehicle drove along.

Markings

The subject of British military markings on Jeeps is far too complex to be covered properly here, but for those who would like to know more, a recommended source is *British Military Markings 1939-1945*, written by Peter Hodges and Michael D Taylor and published in December 1994 by Cannon Publications.

Modification kits

There were several officially approved modification kits. These included an engine-driven compressor (for tyre inflation), a front-mounted capstan winch that was driven from an adaptor fitted to the starter dog, an A-frame hitch on the front bumper, an inter-vehicle starting socket, and a winterisation kit for extremely cold conditions. There also appears to have been a "standard" British wire-cutting kit (although many wire-cutters were improvised in the field out of sheer necessity). This was developed and manufactured to meet an October 1944 Ministry of Supply contract by Duple Motor Bodies of Hendon, who in peace time were makers of luxury coach bodies.

SAS Jeeps

Operating in the Western Desert in 1942, the Special Air Service (then officially the Long Range Desert Group) operated a total of 16 Jeeps that they modified to meet their needs. The main aim was self-sufficiency for the vehicle's two-man crew who might need to operate for several days behind enemy lines. The Jeeps were modified to carry multiple jerrycans of fuel, and some were supposedly fitted with auxiliary tanks. Space was found to stow additional rations, water, ammunition, and of course personal kit. Typically, there would be an expansion tank (an improvised ancestor of the surge tank kit) ahead of the grille, which would have several of its bars cut away to improve cooling in the desert heat. These Jeeps were also heavily armed, partly for self-defence and partly for raiding duties. A typical complement of weaponry was a pair of Vickers K machine guns and a Browning .50 calibre machine cannon.

Quite unmistakable as a British "SAS" Jeep, this one is bristling with weaponry and festooned with supplies for remote operations behind enemy lines. The radiator expansion tank is an improvised type.

APPENDIX B
THE HOTCHKISS M201

At the end of the 1939-1945 war, the US Government presented a total of 22,000 MB and GPW Jeeps to the French government, most of which had belonged to the liberation forces. The objective was ostensibly to allow the French to re-equip their army as quickly as possible, but there was no doubt that the gesture reduced the problem of repatriating large numbers of Jeeps that the US military no longer needed.

Not all of those Jeeps were in serviceable condition, but the French established a fleet by choosing the ones that remained serviceable and by cannibalising others to create a further quantity of serviceable vehicles. They also created a pool of spare parts by breaking up the least easily repairable vehicles and stockpiling the parts they removed. This was only ever intended to be a short-term expedient, and a plan was drawn up to replace these second-hand Jeeps by a purpose-designed vehicle called the VLR. This would be built by the former luxury car manufacturer Delahaye. Unfortunately, Delahaye soon ran into financial difficulties and in 1954 merged with Hotchkiss.

Hotchkiss was another former luxury car maker that had managed to survive in the early post-war period by diversifying. In June 1952, one of its subsidiary companies obtained a licence from Willys in the USA to manufacture both spare parts and complete new vehicles as Willys Overland France. The spare parts business inevitably attracted good custom from the French military and, after the collapse of Delahaye and the end of the VLR project, it led on naturally to a new plan. This time, the French military wanted Hotchkiss to build them complete new Willys MB Jeeps to the original wartime design.

Assembly began during 1955 at the Hotchkiss plant in Saint-Denis, but only 886 were built there before production was moved to a larger factory at Stains, to the north of Paris. Here, manufacture continued at a few thousand a year until 1966, by which time 27,628 (including those first 886) had been made. There were also small numbers of civilian derivatives.

The French-manufactured vehicle was known as an M201. As it was built under licence using the drawings and patterns for the original MB, it is very similar indeed to the American-made wartime Jeep. (Note that the design was based on the Willys original and does not have the variations encountered in the Ford GPW.) Many items are interchangeable. However, over the years Hotchkiss altered the design in some areas to suit French military requirements. For Jeep enthusiasts, it is important to recognise the differences between genuine US-built Jeeps and their Hotchkiss equivalents, not least to avoid buying incorrect parts but also because it is not unknown for unscrupulous sellers in Europe to pass off an M201 as a wartime Jeep, so adding to its apparent market value.

The list of differences that follows here is not claimed to be exhaustive, but should give a good idea of what to look out for. Note that the M201 Jeeps also have their enthusiastic devotees!

Body and fittings

Hotchkiss chose to reinforce the body structure in some areas. The rear body brace beside the seat mountings often has a pair of pressed flutes that are not present on the Willys original. The brace inside the body tub just ahead of the door aperture also has a much more angular shape than the MB type, where the rear edge is curved.

Hotchkiss Jeeps also have metal support hoops mounted to the windscreen top rail instead of support blocks on the bonnet. From 1956 the jerrycan bracket was modified, and from 1960 there were some modifications to body panels.

Lighting and electrics

The first M201 Jeeps had a six-volt electrical system like the MB and GPW, but from some time in 1960 the standard system was changed to a 24-volt type to meet NATO specifications. The 24-volt models have twin 12-volt batteries, the second battery being mounted behind the main battery up against the right-hand inner wing and slightly lower down.

Hotchkiss also fitted electric windscreen wipers that are operated by a single centrally-mounted motor. There is a protective plate along the inside of the windscreen top rail to shield the wiper mechanism.

The reflectors on the rear of the body have a broad circular rim with four mounting holes, as compared to the two mounting holes on genuine MB and GPW Jeeps. From 1960, the headlights were fitted with integral sidelights.

Dash and interior

The Hotchkiss steering wheel differed from the type used on MB and GPW Jeeps in having a larger hub and much wider spokes. It was moulded from black plastic. The Hotchkiss steering column clamp was also bolted to the bulkhead instead of riveted as in the MB and GPW.

The turned-down flange at the top of the dash has very noticeable spot-welds on the Hotchkiss, and does not have the cut-out notch of the MB and GPW models. There are also several differences in the appearance and number of the dashboard switches. The W201 has its starter switch on the dashboard rather than on the floor, and from 1958 it also had the switch for the electric windscreen wipers on the dash. The French data plate is also quite different from those fitted to the MB and GPW models.

The Hotchkiss door safety straps are also larger than the original wartime type, with a width of 5cm (approximately two inches) as compared to 1.5 inches for the originals.

Engine and transmission

Although Hotchkiss continued to use the Willys 134 cubic-inch Go-Devil engine, the French company made a few changes. The earliest engines were pretty well identical to the Willys originals, but a very obvious change made after the M201 had been in production for around a year was that the original Carter carburettor was changed for a Solex type M32 PBIC. The air filter was also relocated on the driver's side of the engine bay, alongside the inner wing.

From early on, the cylinder head was strengthened and a different radiator was fitted, with a new water pump. During 1961, there were changes to the oil filter housing.

There were changes to the transmission as well. During 1956, an improved clutch plate, probably made by original manufacturer Auburn, was fitted. Both primary gearbox and transfer gearbox were strengthened during 1957, when there was a further clutch plate change to one manufactured by Ferodo.

Radiator

French-built radiators also differ from the original type, and can be recognised by the number of holes in the shroud, where there are four instead of the five originally present.

Chassis, suspension and wheels

The chassis frame was built to the Willys pattern, and therefore had a tubular front cross-member. The front bumper also followed the Willys style in having only a starting-handle-hole. However, the front chassis legs on the M201 Jeeps were stiffened by a small U-section channel welded inside each front frame rail at right-angles to it. This is a most distinctive recognition point.

Hotchkiss fitted late-pattern road springs, with ten leaves at the front and 11 leaves at the rear. These springs also had Willys-type leaf clamps made from a single piece of steel strip that was bent over at its top ends.

The French company also made small modifications to the parking brake for the M201, and in 1957 introduced an adjustable steering link. Its pintle hook for the M201 was very similar to the original but was modified by fitting a safety pin that had to be withdrawn before the jaws could be opened.

Early Hotchkiss wheels were made in two pieces attached one to the other by means of rivets. Later wheels had the two halves welded together. Split-rim types were not used. Very early M201s had 6.00 x 16 bar-grip tyres like those on the wartime Jeeps, but later switched to a 6.50 x 16 size, the original suppliers being Goodyear and Kleber.